THE
ALCHEMY
OF
AUTHENTIC
LEADERSHIP

STEVEN MUNDAHL

BALBOA.
PRESS

A DIVISION OF HAY HOUSE

Balboa Press books may be ordered through booksellers or by contacting:

Balboa Press
A Division of Hay House
1663 Liberty Drive
Bloomington, IN 47403
www.balboapress.com
1-(877) 407-4847

Because of the dynamic nature of the Internet, any web addresses or links contained in
this book may have changed since publication and may no longer be valid. The views
expressed in this work are solely those of the author and do not necessarily reflect the
views of the publisher, and the publisher hereby disclaims any responsibility for them.

The author of this book does not dispense medical advice or prescribe the use of any
technique as a form of treatment for physical, emotional, or medical problems without the
advice of a physician, either directly or indirectly. The intent of the author is only to offer
information of a general nature to help you in your quest for emotional and spiritual
well-being. In the event you use any of the information in this
book for yourself, which is your constitutional right, the author and
the publisher assume no responsibility for your actions.

Any people depicted in stock imagery provided by Thinkstock are models,
and such images are being used for illustrative purposes only.
Certain stock imagery © Thinkstock.

ISBN: 978-1-4525-7631-2 (sc)
ISBN: 978-1-452-57632-9 (hc)
ISBN: 978-1-4525-7630-5 (e)

Library of Congress Control Number: 2013910746

Printed in the United States of America.

Balboa Press rev. date: 07/03/2013

To leaders everywhere . . .
who first become leaders of their own lives.

To my brother Phil, a fellow visionary.

CONTENTS

INTRODUCTION

W hy another book about leadership? I've written this book for two reasons. The first is that hardly a day goes by that we don't read about another "outed" leader. Men and women we trust to be ethical and moral enough to represent us as leaders fall because they haven't done the often hard work of self-improvement and therefore fall far short of the definition of an authentic leader. Without the inner work of healing, leaders fall from grace for many reasons, and no segment of society is spared—politics, religion, sports, acting, business, or education.

The second reason is that I have found leadership to be a personal journey. While the demands and responsibilities of leadership are somewhat universal, we all come from positions of authority with different unhealed aspects of our personalities. Our dramas play out in myriad ways, and while my leadership journey is far from complete, I wish to share some of that inner work with you, trusting that it might trigger or mirror what remains unhealed in your personality. If power does one thing to leaders, it heightens our insecurities and accentuates our personal unhealed wounds.

The beginning chapters of this book take us on a journey into our inner homes and guide us through the different rooms of our inner landscapes—family, relationships, health, spirituality, finances, career, creative expression, and enjoyment. As we assess what we find in these rooms, we are asked to make note of the areas in which we find strength and those where we have work to do. In these inner rooms we find historic remnants of our hurts and wounds from childhood. We all have them.

I describe what I term the *BeOUTEDtudes*—a simple play on words that represents some of the landmines of leadership. These are the attitudes and drivers within us that can lead our lives to public ruin and personal disaster. Being "outed" is not just for the movie star or the rogue religious or political figure. The *BeOUTEDtudes* are billboards along the side of our journey's road that offer warnings of unhealed behaviors that could take any of us to ruin.

Since I've spent my life in my inner rooms, I have come to understand that one of life's great missions is to find healing. For me, these acts of correcting moral flaws and childhood insecurities have become the prime focus of my life because these human flaws affect every action and relationship in our lives.

Although I have spent most of my life in leadership roles as a corporate leader, an entrepreneur, and currently a leader in the nonprofit sector, I saw the strong need for collaboration with a skilled professional who could offer healing techniques for those reading this work. While I have become an ardent student of healing modalities, I am not the teacher. Fortunately, the answer was right beside me: my wife, Sharon, who is a skilled psychotherapist of thirty-eight years and a gifted intuitive and corporate coach. I felt a powerful synergy formed by combining my experience as a company president with her professional insights. I feel confident that you will benefit from the insights of both of us.

From the identification of the limiting beliefs, triggers, and addictive behaviors of leaders who self-medicate, Sharon offers us an overview of specific modalities in chapter 5 that address these issues. Case examples of typical healing scenarios of her work with leaders will help you see that healing into wholeness doesn't have to be an overwhelming task. In chapter 6, "Visualization and Pure Intended Thought," I illustrate two of my favorite alchemical tools for leaders with examples from my own life. Chapter 7 is another synergistic chapter written between Sharon and me in which we provide intuitive skill-building exercises and inspirational stories to spark your use of intuition in your company decisions.

From the inspiration of those chapters, we then address the subject of core negative attitudes that still dominate many business cultures. We have all been held hostage by these often debilitating and counterproductive business practices. Where they come from, how they are perpetuated, and most importantly how enlightened, healed leadership can change them as the overall culture of business also comes into a new and exciting age of change.

Finally, the book ends with what I call the *Tenets of Authentic Leadership*. These are the practices and beliefs that have guided my life, and they might be helpful in yours as well. While our learning is never complete and the journeys leading our lives and the lives of others are never over, we can learn to walk the higher road of solid ethics and values. They enter our lives when we rid ourselves of those unwanted practices, those unhealed doubts, and those shortcomings with which we all struggle.

Enjoy the journey.

The Personal Journey of Leadership

Do not follow where the path may lead.
Go instead where there is no path and leave a trail.
—Ralph Waldo Emerson

Once you live a deeply authentic life, leadership will find you rather than you having to wait for it. Others will clearly identify the leader in you, and the trail you blaze will become a beacon to others.

When I thought I was ready to lead a nonprofit agency as a chief executive, I interviewed in three different cities and with three different boards of directors. In the first two interviews, I was so busy presenting my experience and knowledge that I did not give myself the chance to introduce my authentic, more human self for them to get to know. In the third interview, I presented myself very differently. I listened. When asked, I spoke not so much of my experiences in business and leadership but of my experiences in life—the long journey of supporting a wife who battled cancer, my dream to own my own company, and the resulting stress of actually building it. I shared the life changes that had brought me to the doors of failure and the mistakes that made me drop to my knees in humility and surrender. I told of the lessons I had learned as a father of two daughters and of the beauty of the deeply spiritual life I had come to know as I grew older.

I also listened to the board members. I heard that they were looking for someone who was ethical, down-to-earth, and a defender of people with disabilities. They wanted a leader who had been through difficult life experiences and could lead their agency through difficult experiences of its own. I was interviewed three times by two panels of board members and also by management employees of the company. In short, I was offered the presidency of this agency not because I was the strongest fiscal manager or the most educated or even the most experienced, but because I was the most "human" candidate they had interviewed. Many shared that piece of information with me much later. They offered me the keys to the front door of their agency because I had learned some emotionally human principles and could be the ethical leader they sought. Above all, these volunteer community leaders wanted an ethical, caring leader.

Speaking honestly during those interviews allowed me to demonstrate vulnerability and compassion for myself. They saw humanness and authenticity because I chose to share it. They also saw a man who had come to like himself (pretty much) through trial and error. Having a troubled agency, they needed an ethical builder.

Leadership is less about leading others and more about the journey of how we lead ourselves. The task offered to us closely mirrors where we are on our own personal journeys. Life somehow gives us the lessons we need most when it is our best time to learn them. The job isn't so much "out there" as it is "in here." The journey involves finding our truth, our voice, and our passion and then aligning ourselves to them every day.

If we can live from this freshness, others will pick up the trail quite effortlessly.

Over the years, my personal statement of leadership has evolved. The main goal I practice now is to live an ethical life and be an honest leader by practicing spiritual principles without necessarily promoting any religion or brand of spirituality. I attempt to treat others with respect and kindness because of who I see them to be and how I'd like them to see me. My leadership journey helped me realize that I never needed to "go" anywhere on my journey. Leadership found me when I found the leader within myself. I hadn't needed to trek from job to job, progress through layers of middle management, watch scores of years pass me by, learn countless leadership concepts, or even wait for the executive position I desired.

I became my own leader when I started to clean up the negative beliefs about myself that others triggered. I learned to move from a simple overreaction rooted in anger, shame, guilt, or hurt to a healthier pattern. I looked for what triggered me, recognized it, and approached the same situation with clarity and a more positive self. I began by becoming the leader of my own life. It must be an odd statement to read—becoming the leader of your own life—but I believe it really begins there for all of us. As I look back on my journey, I realize that I went through a spiritual evolution as much as a physical or mental one. I felt a fundamental transformation from the man I was to the man I have become. Leadership became the journey, not the destination, and it remains so to this day.

The inner journey I ask you to take is an important step to becoming an authentic leader for two reasons. First, we need to earn and keep the trust extended to us. According to dictionary.com, authenticity is defined as being "entitled to belief because of agreement with known facts . . . to be reliable and trustworthy." In other words, we are entitled to others' trust that we can lead successfully when we begin to live our personal lives with integrity—no acting, no hiding, no running, no denial, no blaming others. Authenticity begins with self-acceptance and matures when we accept our vulnerabilities and the vulnerabilities of those around us.

Secondly, if we are in alignment with our own inner truth, we can acquire a powerful voice to help transform others and our businesses. Our energy becomes focused, clear, and a powerful magnet for good. When we cannot find happiness within, our moral compass goes awry, and we begin to hear the alluring voice of unethical choices.

The following exercise is a way for you to assess yourself. Careful examination of your personal life is similar to analyzing the different inner components or departments of your company. This exercise is similar to the *Wheel of Life* that many personal and business coaches use with their clients. Find a quiet time to do this exercise and assess the different aspects, or rooms, in your life.

A Visit to Your "Inner House"

This leadership journey begins with an assessment of six major life areas. An evaluation of our inner attitudes, values, and habits will help us understand the success or disappointment we feel in these areas of our lives. Ultimately our evaluation will lead us to where we would ideally like our lives to be.

Begin with imagining your ideal home. In your mind, picture where it is. Maybe it is on a beach or a mountaintop. It may be in a foreign country, at the end of a long tree-lined road, or on a tropical white sand beach. Look at its design and color. Is it made of brick, stone, or wood? How many windows face the front, and what size and shape are they? Now imagine walking up to the front door and opening it. As it opens, you are greeted by the owner of this home—you! Your host gives you a warm embrace as though you have just completed a long journey. He or she is delighted to see you. You stand at the doorway just as you are now, looking at yourself as the successful, beloved leader you will become. Each room of this ideal home is filled with the accomplishments of your efforts, a culmination of a life of commitment and service. The leader you see as yourself has an accepting, loving, and confident presence.

Within this home, you find a holographic image that shifts between two interchangeable houses. From one angle, you can see that one of the houses is somewhat less complete than the other. That is the home you currently occupy. From another angle, the home is wonderfully complete. It is finished in every detail, with rooms filled to potential and overflowing with abundance. It holds everything that would make you feel that your life has been lived with great fulfillment.

The Inner Rooms

These are the rooms of your life. There are no walls that separate them, for they flow naturally together. For our purposes, we will discuss them as separate rooms, although you will see how one affects the other and how easily these rooms can overlap. For our exercise, there are six rooms in all:

1. Money and finances
2. Leisure, creativity, and fun
3. Spirituality and philosophy

4. Career and education
5. Family and relationships
6. Physical and emotional health

Together, we will enter each room and take notice of its current contents and the condition in which it appears to you today. You will also have the opportunity to describe how you would like the room to look in your finished house. As you compare the current look of the room to the potential of what it could be, I will ask you to make note of the differences. You will then simply grade the room from one to five, with five being the highest level of personal satisfaction.

Within these rooms are habits, practices, and values you use every day. If you find a room lacking in use or potential, ask yourself why that is. Conversely, you may find a room already overflowing with activity and abundance. Take note of why. Later we will examine principles that might change the capacity, energy, and potential of each room.

Your tour guide is your wise, successful, accepting self—that authentic leader you have become. This tour is purely personal. Relax and take your time. Remember, no self-judgment is allowed. We begin with the room of money and finances, but we don't begin here because it is the most important. The rooms used in this model have no hierarchy other than the level of importance and satisfaction you place upon them at any given time.

Money and Finances

As you stand at the closed door of this room, how do you feel about opening it to honestly reveal its condition? Make a note of this feeling and then proceed to open the door. Now, within this room make some mental notes on all you see or don't see.

- Are you making enough?
- Do you live paycheck to paycheck?
- Do you feel you have too much debt?
- Do you live on a cash-on-hand basis or have a habit of charging on credit cards?
- Do you have a savings plan?
- What value and importance do you place on money and finances?
- Do you experience any secret shame when it comes to money?
- Do you have difficulty living within your budget while others seem to have all the "extras"?
- Do you even feel that you are entitled to be wealthy?

We live in a society that is extremely focused on money. It is a widely, though not necessarily wisely, used standard to determine success and a life of completion. Our economic and social culture in business today can promote greed and self-indulgence in leadership, although it is certainly not always so. I recently heard that 90 percent of the world's wealth is concentrated in the hands of 1 percent of the population, and the gulf between rich and poor grows wider each year. Most of the wealth lies in the hands of leaders. Much of the outrage of the Wall Street and other financial protests in recent years has been at the greed and imbalance of the wealth at the top.

Take a few moments and record both the condition of your financial house and some of the attitudes and values you currently hold. Remember not to offer judgment of yourself. You are far from alone.

_____

_____

_____

Your Ideal Money and Finances Room

Take a moment now and shift your vision to the holographic view of what this area of your life ideally looks like in your completed home.

- What does it look like to have your financial house in order?
- In this ideal fiscal room of your house, what are your highest financial priorities?
- How does it feel to have a date in mind for your debt to be paid off or to actually have it all paid off?
- What kind of a savings plan have you either started or increased?
- Is there any kind of training or advancement plan you have begun that will lead to even greater financial security?
- What kind of inner peace do you now have from greater security?
- If you could turn on a faucet of abundance in your life, how much money would take you to the place called "success?" Would you spend freely, invest it, or give it away as it flowed to you?

Take a moment and briefly describe your results.

_____

_____

_____

On a scale of one to five, with five being quite satisfied, rate the condition of this room in your life right now: _____.

Take a moment and record a few priorities to address in this room.

_____

_____

_____

Leisure, Creativity, and Enjoyment

In this room are your hobbies, creative interests, talents, and desire to invent, produce, and create. Here also is where you enjoy yourself the most. In this room you can laugh and play like a kid. This is where you create, write, paint, play music, travel, and read your favorite novels. This room is where you get in touch with your uniqueness, that which excites and inspires you. This is where you tap into your unique tastes, talents, and preferences. As you stand at the closed door of this room, how do you feel about opening it to honestly reveal its condition? Make a note of this and then proceed to open the door. As you step into this room, how would you describe how much time you spend on enjoyable activities here?

- Do you have regular classes or time devoted to leisure or creative endeavors?

- Are there paintings here, poems you have written, musical instruments you have practiced?
- Are there songs you have written or perhaps a novel you have started?
- Has life become too busy for this room, or are you satisfied with the energy and time you spend here?
- Are you a bit of a workaholic and emphasize getting everything done over and above pure enjoyment of life's pleasures?
- Do you have peer relationships in which you pursue mutual hobbies or sports?
- Do you have time to simply enjoy the beauty of nature, music, art, and exercise apart from work?
- Do you have any yearly memberships that enforce getting out and being active in enjoying the arts, exercise, or worthwhile causes?

When American viewers saw President Bill Clinton playing the saxophone and laughing on late-night television, they were amazed. How could such an important leader spend time being so frivolous? It begs the question, should leaders have fun in the workplace? Should they allow employees and constituents to have fun as well? Millennial companies such as Google and Yahoo are filled with young workers in their twenties and early thirties and have demonstrated that fun needs to be an important part of the business day. How much fun and creativity are you allowed in your workplace, if any? How much fun and creative expression do you allow in your day?

A European friend of mine recently told me that European workers, on average, take almost twice the number of vacation days as American workers, all while American workers are believed to be working longer hours in 2012 than in any other decade of our history, often foregoing vacations completely. Personal job satisfaction ranks at its lowest level in decades. One in four American adults is taking antidepressants, and more than half of the population of the country is overweight. Are we happier for the excess work hours? Are we living more fulfilling lives than our parents or grandparents?

Take a moment and make some notes about how you feel about the fun and creativity you are having in your life and the amount of time you are giving to leisure or creative endeavors.

Your Ideal Leisure, Creativity, and Fun Room

Take a moment now to shift your vision to the fulfilled holographic vision of this room. How does this room look filled with fun, leisure activities, and creative endeavors you have long sought to accomplish? Perhaps you have written a novel and are signing books to long lines of readers. Perhaps you are becoming known for your music, poetry, acting, or sculpting. Or perhaps you are simply able to make homemade gifts for people or teach a class on your hobby.

In this room of your house, picture your staff enjoying hearing about your latest hobbies and interests and feeling encouraged to have more fun and balance in their own lives. Imagine the pride you feel in being a well-rounded, versatile leader. Feel the bounce in your step and the anticipation you feel looking forward to certain activities. Make some notes.

On a scale of one to five, rate how satisfied you are with the condition of this room in your life right now _____.
List three priorities to address.

Spirituality and Philosophy

Your room of spirituality is your home of religion, philosophy, and the deep inner beliefs you hold as truth. Here you will find your values and ethics and your belief in life beyond this human experience. Before you enter the closed door of this room, how do you feel about entering it? Are you satisfied? Do you sense a bit of longing or even guilt? As you enter this room, answer these questions:

- What importance does this room play in your life?
- How satisfied are you with your daily or weekly religious or spiritual practices?
- Have your views changed over time?
- Have you developed a deeper conviction in your belief, or do you find yourself still searching for meaning?
- Is your spiritual life deeply integrated in your personal and business life, or do you hold it separate?
- Do you spend time with a group of individuals who share and support the integration of your spiritual principles into daily life?

Finding ways to develop a greater love of self and others as we might believe the Creator loves us is part of the spiritual assignment given to all of us. Ultimately this room will play an important role in your leadership journey, if it hasn't already. It is often a place where you can find intense energies within you, some negative and others positive and profound. Here is the seat of prejudice, righteousness, and your sense of right and wrong— your conscience. Here also you will find your inner voice.

In my journey to find meaning, I abandoned much of my childhood teachings and studied various religions and philosophical ways to define life. I finally arrived at a basic premise that I could live my life on, one statement that could define who I was and what purpose my life had. A bumper sticker I saw once sums up that definition very nicely: *I am a spiritual being having a human experience, not a human being having a spiritual experience.* Once I understood that my essence was spiritual, I could shrug off religious beliefs that made no sense to me and find my own path. This had once been the emptiest room in my life, but over time it has become quite the opposite. Our relationships to the Creator, whatever concept that might be for you, are often how we learn to relate to others. How we feel the Creator cares for us is often how we project our own brand of self-care and care for others.

Presidents and political leaders often speak of their faith, but business leaders often sidestep the issue completely. In my life, leadership and spirituality became a merged journey. Once I felt that the Universe and its Creator loved and accepted me as I was, I started treating myself better and practiced being kinder to myself. How we treat ourselves is quickly reflected in how we treat others.

Your Ideal Spirituality and Philosophy Room

Now step back into the holographic vision of the completed spiritual room where you have realized a high level of spiritual satisfaction.

- What role does your spiritual life play in your home of ultimate success and happiness?
- What kind of community do you sense is supporting you? Is it different than the one you have now?

- What kind of spiritual relationship do you have with your mate or significant other?
- Do you have any daily or weekly spiritual or philosophical practices (reading inspirational books, meditation, prayer, or positive affirmations that you do alone or together to bring you into a higher positive state, closer to your higher self)?
- What role does your spiritual life play in your leadership journey?

Make some notes for yourself.

Now, on a scale of one to five, rate how satisfied you are with the condition of this room in your life right now:_____. List three priorities to address issues in this room.

Career and Education

Before you enter the closed door to this room, how do you feel? Are you happy to review the contents and accomplishments? Now as you enter the room devoted to your career and education, ask yourself some important questions: Am I doing the work that is fulfilling to me? Does it have a positive impact on others? Do I feel passion in what I do, or has my career become routine and unfulfilling?

Most of us will work forty to fifty years in our lives. More than a third of the hours we live will be spent working. The hours we spend at our jobs will occupy the best part of every day and forge some of our strongest relationships.

I have two grown daughters who have reminded me of how many times I made them pack up their belongings, say good-bye to their friends, and move to another town or state so that I might find some happiness and fulfillment in my career. I worked in sales, and although I was good at what I did, I never felt fully satisfied with my career choice. As I reflect now, I felt some inner push to keep marching from job to job, employer to employer. Some part of me wanted more and wasn't going to allow me to settle down until I found a different career path. While selling is a vitally important career, it was not aligned with my inner purpose. It wasn't until my children were older that I learned how upsetting all of these moves had been in their lives.

I was fifty years old before my career path changed and really became known to me. I hope you won't have to labor for so long. Since finding Goodwill and nonprofit leadership, I have enjoyed much success, been happier than at any other time in my life, and have moved only once, and that was to take leadership of my own agency. While company problems exist, I lie down every night knowing I have made life a little bit better for others. It is a good and deeply satisfying feeling.

I heard Michael Jordan once comment to a reporter, "Sometimes I just can't believe how fortunate I have been to make such a great living at something which is so enjoyable and fun for me to do." Isn't that a wonderful statement? Can we imagine saying that? We all can't make millions as a professional athlete, but we can work at jobs that fulfill our purpose and energize our lives.

Once my career path was in alignment with my values, I became unstoppable in reaching my goals. The alignment between my heart's desire and my chosen profession energized me so much that I couldn't get to president and CEO fast enough. I returned to college and finished my master's degree, took the executive development path that was offered through Goodwill, learned all I could from my employer and our nonprofit team, and set out to become the leader of my own agency.

No matter how many years it takes you to develop a career that allows you to make a ugood living while doing meaningful work for yourself and others, don't regret any employment you have had; all experiences have prepared you in many ways.

Take a moment and make notes on where you are today in your education and career:

- Does your career turn up the volume and increase the vibration of your life?
- Do you feel passion in what you do, or has your career become routine and unfulfilling?
- Is there any kind of training you need that would enhance job satisfaction and career goals?
- Are there any steps you need to take to discuss career satisfaction or educational goals with your employer?
- Do you need to reach out to other leaders on a regular basis to get stimulating new ideas or improve problem solving and emotional support?
- Do you feel passionate about your career, and if not, what changes do you need to make?
- Are you making an impact on the world in the way you desire?
- Who are your role models, and what could you do to emulate those leaders?

Your Ideal Career and Education Room

Now view the holographic image of your completed room and make some notes about your perfect career.

- What is your position, and how much do you make?
- Paint the perfect career portrait for yourself, and for the moment, see yourself as already there. How does it

make you feel? Are you pursuing your desire? Are you affecting the world or community around you?

- Do you have a support network and further educational opportunities that you need to do your job?
- Can you picture a great relationship with your board of directors and staff?
- Are you a leader in any cutting-edge efforts to improve conditions for those less fortunate or those in adverse conditions in the world?
- What are the headlines in the paper about your accomplishments?

As you reflect on your career choice and what you do today, rate the level of satisfaction of this room in your life on a scale of one to five. Record your score here: _____.

List three priorities to address issues in this room.

Family and Relationships

Of all the lessons we learn in life, family and relationships teach us the most. Whether we come from a strong and loving family or from a highly dysfunctional one, most of our life lessons spring from this environment. Here dwell our most important mentors, our deepest hurts and wounds, our most precious memories, and also our greatest fears. From family and personal relationships we ask searching questions and seek lasting answers. Am I good enough, pretty enough, talented enough? Am I lovable or loving enough, nurturing enough, playful enough, patient enough, kind enough?

We spend much of our adult lives expressing the many talents learned and attempting to heal wounds from childhood.

We bring them into our marriages, our workplaces, and our friendships. We carry them visibly and invisibly. Authentic leadership requires us to express and share our talents while healing hurts and wounds from our childhood if we are to succeed in accepting ourselves and to ultimately succeed in leadership.

Leadership skills are fundamentally relationship skills. Here is where the journey can be the richest and most rewarding while also the loneliest and most intensely personal. If we attempt to hide our insecurities, they will inevitably show up, perhaps even with consequences, such as when we are fired or publicly "outed." If we have developed the skill of using our relationships as a catalyst for personal development and growth, however, the same skills translate effectively into leadership. For example, it may well be that an individual who would cheat on his or her mate would also be a candidate for cheating the company and employees. A person that will hide the truth from a mate might also hide the truth from the board of directors or employees. It is the act of hiding and cheating that makes the difference, not the environment in which we choose to act.

I married when I returned from the war in Vietnam, before really understanding the purpose of relationships. I was lonely from almost a year away from home. Without giving myself time for personal growth or adjustment, I quickly threw myself into marriage and family. I had not yet learned that the purpose of a relationship with another person is to offer us a reflection of our own issues and therefore areas for growth, just as a mirror reflects the image of our faces. I found myself veering at times into pursuits and activities that were not healthy or fair to my mate instead of doing the inner work required of me. I took years to learn and gain the courage to correct this in my life, and I left some pain behind when I finally did. If the inner work is not done, we can go from relationship to relationship, but the personal reflection doesn't change, and the same drama is often played out with partner after partner. Partners trigger our insecurities and childhood hurts and therefore play a vital role for healing when we become aware of this.

Courage in leadership is a reflection of courage learned in relationships. When we learn to live our lives in truth and honesty, we step into authentic leadership, and we make our own trail for others to follow. Too many of us have worked for leaders who lack courage—one of the core values of servant leadership. Those who fail miserably in personal relationship traits can also fail in business relationships.

Before you enter the closed door of your family and relationship room, how do you feel about honestly looking at its contents and the satisfaction found there? Make some notes about the role of relationships in your life and how healthy and satisfying they are to you, or how they reflect the work you should be doing to live in truth and act with courage.

- Are you honest in your significant relationships?
- Are you open to hearing honest feedback from others?
- Are you able to receive as well as give love and nurturing?
- Are you able to reach out and admit you need help or emotional support?
- Are you addressing any issues, including receiving professional help if your relationship has lost some of its intimacy and fulfillment?
- Do you have any deceitful behaviors?
- What triggers your emotional issues in a relationship? Do you know their causes or origins?

Your Ideal Family and Relationships Room

Now view the holographic image of this completed room.

- Perhaps you live with your ideal mate now. What are you doing to keep the vibrant energy and intimacy alive? Feel the satisfaction in having learned from all the issues raised in relationships.
- You may have clarity on which action to take in a relationship and great peace of mind.
- You may see yourself setting more boundaries now where they are needed.
- You may be skilled at seeing any overreaction to others as issues from your past you have now addressed.
- Perhaps you have not found your ideal mate; however, you are feeling ready and know that eventually you will find the one who makes you feel supported, loved, cherished, whole, and successful.

Pause for a moment and record your thoughts. From one to five, rate how satisfied you are with your mate or important relationships: _____.

List three priorities to address issues in this room.

Physical and Emotional Health

As you enter this room, take a moment to assess your physical and emotional health. These are core values in leadership, and they play roles greater than most people will ever realize. Leadership will challenge your health systems in unique ways.

Habits such as drinking, smoking, and lack of physical exercise will affect the core strength of your leadership. Emotional health is also vitally important to authentic leaders who learn to manage themselves in balanced, healthy routines and emotional well-being.

In college, I was a pretty good soccer player for my junior college and was in excellent physical condition. In the Marine Corps, I grew even stronger. I remember being able to do sit-ups until I wished to stop—an almost uncountable number! Oh, how the years have changed that! At fifty, I was seventy pounds heavier! Aches and pains were part of my day, and I was cautioned more than once at my annual physical exams about health issues such as elevated cholesterol and high blood pressure. I knew I needed change, but it wasn't until I really began to see that my emotional well-being was not in a healthy place that I found the discipline to make the outer physical changes.

If you need to get some physical habits under control—weight, smoking, drinking, shopping, or escaping too much with video games, the Internet, or other pursuits that take you away from your leadership journey—stop and assess your emotional health. It is the foundation upon which your physical health is built. Correct the issues there first, and you will find the discipline to stop bad habits and get control of your life. Trying to correct physical changes without a change in emotional issues can be a most frustrating experience. Leadership begins by being a strong and healthy leader in your own life.

Emotional health assessment has finally made it to the board room and executive offices of many companies, but it took a painfully long time to recognize that the health of our emotional systems are a vital function of healthy leadership. This is equally true for the emotional health of your business. Many leadership books discuss how to treat employees to receive maximum return, but I believe it begins with how leaders learn to treat themselves. For too long we have maintained that leaders must be cool, unemotional, even-tempered, and closed to the emotional needs of their employees and customers. I disagree. We need to be able to take the emotional pulse of ourselves as well as our employees.

Recently I saw a big-city mayor weeping as he walked through his tornado-devastated city neighborhoods. His sleeves were rolled up, his shirt was dirty, and he freely wept as he met friends and fellow citizens who had lost homes and loved ones. Was it a sign of weakness or a sign of strong, caring, and emotionally healthy leadership?

Record how satisfied you are with your emotional and physical well-being.

- How healthy are you? Do you work out regularly, walk, swim, or participate in some other regular physical activity?
- How successful are you at maintaining your stress level, healthy diet, and weight?
- Do you notice and tend to your own feelings throughout the day?
- Are you your best friend when it comes to being positive and unconditionally accepting of yourself?
- Are most of your friends positive and upbeat?
- Are you able to express your honest emotional feelings to others when appropriate?

Your Ideal Physical and Emotional Health Room

Now return to the holographic view of this ideal room. If you could paint a perfect healthy picture of yourself, what would it look like?

- Are you continuing your current exercise program, or do you see that you have a new exercise program that has become second nature to you?
- Are you incorporating exercise and stress reduction throughout the day?
- Are people complimenting you on your vibrant looks?
- Are you beginning to take your good health for granted and see this as an essential priority in having true happiness in life?
- Perhaps you are already physically fit. Would you be competitive in a marathon or ski the best runs in January with ease?
- Did you receive life coaching, counseling, or psychotherapy when you felt you needed motivation, insight, additional tools, and emotional support?

Take a moment to record your thoughts.

On a scale of one to five, with five being the most satisfied, take a moment to rate your overall health, physically and emotionally as they are now in your life: _____. List three priorities to address issues in this room.

Summarizing Your Home Tour

You've been through a long and important journey in your inner home. Simply stated, effective leadership begins at home. It starts by getting off the path others tell you to walk and making your own trail. A sloppy personal life can lead to a sloppy leadership style. The workaholic leader is not always an effective one because he or she tends to micromanage others rather than trusting in their abilities to also lead. A life out of balance with spirit and faith can lead to moral failures in the workplace. Families need not suffer at the expense of career, and neither should creative, physical, or spiritual endeavors be slighted. Taking the time for an annual self-analysis should provide you with the insight necessary for change. You are deserving of fulfillment, happiness, and as balanced a life as you are capable of creating!

Add up the scores you gave yourself in each room. Compare those scores with the summary below:

- Twenty-five to thirty points—Congratulations! You are quite satisfied with how you are living your life.
- Twenty to twenty-five points—Some work is needed! Your leadership journey has a few potholes to fill, but you're well on your way.
- Less than twenty points—Road construction time! It is time to begin some new habits and make some needed changes.

Did the results surprise you? Was the exercise difficult or easy? In the next chapter, we will begin to work with the core issues that define you. If you put the effort into making healthy changes now, they will become the excellent preparation for your leadership journey.

CHAPTER

2

Leadership Begins at Home

Knowing yourself is the beginning of all wisdom.
—Aristotle

I t is time to answer an important question: how much do you *really* believe that you can have any of your wonderful visions in your ideal home—the desired amount of money, fulfilling relationships, creative outlets, satisfying career, and meaningful spiritual life? On a scale of one to five (with five being the highest belief), write your truthful answer right here: _____.

When you find your leader within, you will begin to reflect those leadership qualities to others. It takes courage. It takes discipline. It takes commitment. When you begin, however, the energy for change will come. It just takes a beginning.

In the areas where your answers were less than five in the last chapter, ask yourself why you do not have fulfillment in these areas. Who or what is holding your back? No one is really stopping us from our success, of course. There are challenges galore, but there is no grand conspiracy to keep us from realizing our vision for a great life. In fact, our visions are the directives from our higher selves that we need to honor.

These visions are what truly excite and inspire us and what will eventually lead us to leave our marks on the world.

Filling the Gap

Why then do we procrastinate, stay in situations that do not serve us, and not apply ourselves to achieving our desires? The answer may lie in a lack of faith in our own basic worth, in our own abilities, in a multitude of negative life experiences that have dampened our spirits, or simply in a stressful lifestyle that lessens our willpower. When we settle for less, we create a "happiness gap" that we are then naturally motivated to fill. We usually fill it with substitutes: overeating, shopping ourselves into deep debt, gambling, drinking, pornography, and affairs, to name a few. These can compassionately be viewed as attempts to fill that gap, but they can lead to addictive lifestyles. Your focus becomes getting an immediate high in anything but an authentic, wholesome way.

The Foundation of Change: Honesty

Leadership isn't a position to obtain; it is a way of approaching life that has to start within one's conscience, one's core of being. We start with the belief that it is an act of great self-love to be honest with ourselves and a great service to be honest with others. We need to practice asking for honesty from ourselves and then from others. This foundational start of speaking our truth will facilitate our ability to avoid behaviors that will ultimately sabotage our true happiness and success. We learn the fine line between healthy risk and unhealthy risk. Leaders will always take risks, but the risks must be calculated and led to a positive long-term goal.

As leaders, we have to make tough decisions. We carefully analyze what departments in our lives are working and what has served its purpose and requires change, diligence, and adjustment. We adopt the courage and commitment to reinvent ourselves and get busy directing the necessary changes in our lives. As authentic leaders, we learn first to manage our own lives based in honesty and alignment with our core values. We are supposed to lead and solve problems, not be the problem! We need to practice daily transparency with our feelings, thoughts, and wishes beginning with ourselves. I also believe that we need to be a bit of a research psychologist to understand the science of how we either sabotage or achieve success.

Changing Areas in Your Life

After self-analysis in your rooms, along with possibly talking to a friend or advisor, it may be necessary to change a situation in an area of your life that is imbalanced. What is right for you invariably will set others on a path that will ultimately be good for them. For example, if you are unhappy in your relationship, your mate invariably has dissatisfaction as well. Take the initiative to express honest thoughts about your concerns with others. It is always good to express thoughts of your contribution to the problem first! Your actions may create a domino effect. Your heartfelt communication may increase the same in your whole household or worksite. True strength is the ability to be honest and vulnerable with yourself and others.

If you found a high level of satisfaction in all your rooms, relax and know that you are doing a great job. However, don't relax totally; your needs and desires are always changing. The only two constants in life are change and free will. Thank goodness we are ever expanding in our thinking, our abilities, and our need for new and different creative efforts! If we don't listen to our truth of what no longer serves us and our truth of what new endeavors would inspire us, we rightfully will feel a lack in our lives. This insufficiency leaves a gap that is going to call out to us to be filled. Living a life of turning toward false highs and short-term satisfactions to fill the gap is a sure way to being outed! And just in case you need to be reminded of this, I will now speak on . . .

What Happens When You Don't!

Anthony Weiner was a rising star in New York politics—a young, aggressive, intelligent seven-term congressman who some thought was on track to be the next governor. During interviews on major networks, he vehemently denied "sexting" explicit photos of himself to young women he had "met" on Facebook. Under pressure to resign, he finally admitted to sending the photos, which ended his career.

Herman Cain was a rising GOP star. The CEO of Godfather's Pizza had overcome huge obstacles in life to rise to a position of prominence in the business world. He stunned the American political landscape when he entered the race for the Republican nomination for president. He was a powerful, successful black businessman running on a conservative platform, and almost overnight he jumped to the top of the crowded field of GOP presidential hopefuls. During this campaign, allegations of sexual misconduct with several women surfaced, including the allegation of a long-term extramarital affair. Consulting with and under pressure from his party, he chose to withdraw his candidacy.

Senator John Edwards and former California Governor Arnold Schwarzenegger both admitted to living double lives, fathering children outside their marriages. Numerous high-profile religious leaders have also been outed, including Ted Haggard, who frequently condemned homosexuality to his large congregation while living a double life with a male prostitute. Most recently, General David Petraeus, head of the CIA, admitted to an extramarital affair that had been quietly investigated by the FBI. Once outed, the retired general had little choice but to resign.

There probably isn't one of us who hasn't been outed at some time in our lives. Perhaps as children we were caught taking a package of gum from the store without paying for it or telling a lie to our parents only to be caught and made to confess the truth later. As we grow older, the pain, embarrassment, and shame can become magnified many times from our antics as children. If you've been outed" as an adult, you know how painful an "outing" can be. It can cause divorce, loss, public humiliation, embarrassment, and even jail time in extreme cases.

When we see another fallen leader, we can feel relief that it wasn't us. We scan our lives for similar issues and feel uncomfortable if we have something deceptive and potentially embarrassing. In truth, the ones who fall are doing us a service. Perhaps instead of focusing on them in a negative way we should compassionately think, *This soul must have been tired of living in self-deception. Perhaps his or her higher self might have seen that the only way to stop was to be outed. Now he or she has an opportunity for an authentic life of honesty.* We may even add, *What a grand gesture this soul has made!* Their archetypal "fall on the sword" serves as a wake-up call for all of us!

For some of us who are stuck in negative cycles of routine, negative feedback loops, or destructive behavior, it may take a car accident, an ill-timed DUI, or an affair that is discovered by a spouse. It even may take a diagnosis of cancer or a debilitating heart attack when we need to be outed for staying in negative situations or not taking care of ourselves sufficiently.

Most of us are usually in some form of denial about getting caught. Denial can range from *I know it is not the best behavior to take, but I deserve this reward* or *I won't get caught, I am very careful, I drive careful even when drinking, I only spend so much on gambling (even if my overall losses are huge), I don't leave a paper trail, or I act with discretion.* The news has brought you all kinds of almost unbelievable examples of denial and secrecy, from Jerry Sandusky to Arnold Schwarzenegger. Their public embarrassment doesn't seem to prevent others from going down similar steep slopes. Denial is strong! What does it take to wake up? For some, it obviously takes a lot!

What Would Your Headline Be?

The list of risky behaviors is long: drinking and driving, gambling, online or in-person affairs, shoplifting, embezzlement, and the "overs"—spending, eating, shopping, smoking, pornography, drinking. Here are a few questions for you to consider:

- If it were your picture in your local newspaper for everyone to see, what would the headline say?
- If this secret were revealed to your board of directors or your employees, what would it do to you?
- If your spouse, best friend, or children were to find out the secret you are hiding, how would you feel?

Perhaps, with relief, your hidden behaviors would require no headline. For others, how embarrassing or devastating would the revelation of this secret be, whether it happened once or might be revealed to have been happening for years? Ask yourself why you are taking these risks.

It Takes an Attitude . . .

For starters, it takes a certain kind of "attitude" to be outed! Instead of doing our own inner work to have a healthy psyche or practicing self-awareness to boost our self-control, we dangerously rationalize with a healthy list of attitudes that I call the *BeOUTEDtudes!*

The BeOUTEDtudes

- Blessed are the hard workers . . . who then "deserve" rewards of forbidden treats!
- Blessed are the risk takers . . . who rationalize that they need the "high" that risk gives!
- Blessed are the defiant . . . who say damn the consequences!
- Blessed are the privileged . . . who believe they are entitled and above the law!
- Blessed are the brilliant . . . who really believe everyone else's stupidity!
- Blessed are the egotistical . . . whose self-importance knows no bounds.
- Blessed are the blameless . . . who really think "the devil" made me do it!"

- Blessed are the almighty powerful . . . who have the right to mess with others' lives!
- Blessed are the righteous . . . who believe it's "my way or the highway!"
- Blessed are the "bored" . . . who live for excitement in all the wrong places!
- Blessed are the "perfect" ones . . . who refuse to admit their faults.
- Blessed are the vengeful . . . who believe that they have the right to get even!
- Blessed are the important ones . . . who feel their positions entitle them to "perks."

Question the Reward

These and many other attitudes are what put us at risk. The short-term fixes we engage in are sadly corrupting the very fibers of our beings. We are but faint shadows of what we could be if we took a path of mastery of ourselves. If we learn anything from others being outed, it is to want more for ourselves than the tragic ending that normally follows. The behavior might feel good for the moment, but it almost always leads to guilt, regret, remorse, or worse.

Realistically, we are already internally outed the minute we perform the risky or addictive behavior. Guilt, shame, embarrassment, self-talk, remorse—these are all internal reminders that we are not living in accordance with our true values. When we hear the soft murmurings of our conscience, feel the hangover, or experience the pain of overspending, we are feeling the consequences.

I recently heard an actor describe how he prepares for a role, even a small role, in which this actor seems to specialize. He said that in preparation for the role, he always asked himself two questions:

- What is the greatest reward I could possibly receive by playing this part?
- What is my greatest fear?

Think about this for a moment. If you are partaking in risky, possibly even dangerous behaviors, ask yourself those two questions:

- What is the greatest reward I could receive from taking the risk?
- What is my greatest fear?

The Big Question: Why?

Why do these powerful public figures, both men and women, make these choices? Didn't Mr. Weiner, with all his resources and intelligence, have the ability to listen to his inner warning voice, his conscience, and not sabotage his career? Did Tiger Woods have to cavort with several women in a shaming public media saga that ultimately ended his marriage and tarnished his reputation as perhaps the world's greatest golfer? Where did the inner voice go that could have prompted him to look at his infidelity, his risk-taking behavior gone awry?

Who would consciously risk leaving a negative legacy? It undoubtedly takes a Molotov cocktail of some or all of the following: a vibrational gap, unhealed emotional wounds (impaired limits of entitlement or grandiosity, insufficient self-control or discipline, etc.), alcohol or drug use, denial, and miscalculation of risks. We can point fingers and shake our heads at the scandalous actions of public figures, but there is probably not one of us who is not packing one of the ingredients of the Molotov cocktail in some area of his or her life. Together, these impaired attitudes and behaviors acted out long enough will create enough friction to light the Molotov cocktail.

Many leaders will freely admit that they are risk takers. Risk is usually a trait that brings individuals into positions of leadership in the first place. Executives who are hired because of their ability and desire to take risk are often prone to taking risks in other aspects of their lives, including relationships, stealing, fraud, and the "implied" privilege of the positions they hold. But why would powerful men and women such as General David Petraeus risk everything to cheat?

Miscalculation of Risk

Psychologists who study risky behavior in leadership say that falls from grace such as those of Tiger Woods, Schwarzenegger, and Petraeus occur because of "miscalculation" of risk. With power comes privilege. With privilege comes temptation. Baruch Fischhoff of Carnegie Mellon University said in a recent Yahoo news report,

> People tend to underestimate how quickly small risks mount up because of repeated exposure to those risks. You do something once and you get away with it—certain things you're probably

going to get away with because of your risk-taker nature, but you keep doing them often enough and, eventually, the risk gets pretty high. (Yahoo! News, Nov. 12, 2012).

These high risk takers may also have unchecked self-important tendencies that hinder their ability to see the real truth of the hurtfulness or risk of their actions.

Interestingly, although not totally surprising, many powerful men may become blind to risk when an attractive woman enters the picture. Michael Baker, a professor at Eastern Carolina University, recently said,

The risk of losing one's career or reputation is "nothing" compared with the evolutionary drive to reproduce. In that sense, while embarking on an affair may seem inadvisable, even self-destructive, it actually shows something even more powerful called "mating intelligence." Some of these individuals with very high-status, high-power positions have obtained these positions solely for the purpose of attracting reproductive success and to attract more mates. (Yahoo! News, Nov.12, 2012.)

In other studies, men who were shown a picture of a seductive and pretty woman prior to making business decisions were more likely to make poor and risky ones.

There is another important consideration when considering why leaders risk in moral choices. Business CEOs are quite often seen as potential "targets" by subordinates, just as movie stars or rock stars are seen as prospective powerful conquests by those near to them. Individuals willing to take risks in relationships can "hunt out" powerful business leaders because they are often objects "worthy" of taking risks with.

It is worth noting that in years past, business leaders, politicians, and generals could succeed in risky moral behaviors because it was more likely accepted as normal or a privilege of power by those around them; therefore, it was excused, hidden, or disguised. Not so in today's society. Women's rights have highlighted this double standard long held by men. No matter what position is held, even the United States presidency, as in the case of Bill Clinton, transparency has become razor thin, increasing the odds of detection and scrutiny by others.

The Vibrational "Gap"

Almost everyone has heard phrases like "being in the zone" or "feeling whole." These terms conjure up a sense of being in alignment with what excites, inspires, and honors one's truth, talents, and values. Leaders will find it useful to actually picture a vibrational gap that widens if something is pulling their vibration downward. A feeling of depression, lethargy, or desire to leave the office a few hours early, or any number of other "signs," can signal a gap. Life is about continual reevaluation and reinvention, which I will cover in the next section. Leaders need to continually monitor their vibrational levels and make a plan of corrective action instead of turning to the "overs." A craving for alcohol, gambling, affairs, or excessive shopping can then be seen simply as a warning buzzer, like hitting a highway rumble strip signals the need for a course correction.

The Brain Science of Poor Decision Making

Knowing how our brains work under stress is essential to understanding why leaders take risks that can get them fired or put them in scandalous situations. When something new and interesting is happening, we are alert and interested. Even the uncertainty of how something will turn out gives us a feeling of intensity, of pleasure. Simply put, we like to be surprised! We like the "high" we get with the new, the different, the conquest, and the unknown outcome. When we achieve our conquest and the experience becomes commonplace, we lose that intense pleasure.

The term *hedonic adaptation* is used to describe the pleasure and excitement of something new wearing off. You may have heard that some people who win the lottery will have a surge of pleasure and excitement only to have their emotions level off in the months following the win. The degree of life satisfaction remains similar to life before they won. In the beginning stages of courtship and marriage, you have enough novelty to trigger the brain's neurotransmitter dopamine for a real "high." It lasts on average about two years. "This is important to consider for those tempted by extramarital affairs—less than 25% of relationships that begin as an affair last beyond a couple of years, and the concept of hedonic adaptation can help explain why" (Dana Fillmore, "You Probably Have Hedonic Adaptation" Couples Therapy, Marriage Advice December 18, 2012, http://www.strongmarriagenow.com)

Since so many leaders get outed for extramarital affairs, let's look at an example. You are feeling a loss of interest in your spouse. Things feel somewhat humdrum. Your spouse seems unhappy and dissatisfied as well. You even begin to resent coming home and having expectations placed upon you.

It is easier to stay at work in the pleasant company of others, particularly of a staff member of the opposite sex with whom everything is easy and playful.

If you have the scientific self-awareness that the normal "high" in any relationship lasts for approximately two years, you may instead look within your current relationship for new activities, spiritual time together, and honest communication to keep the intimacy alive. Dissatisfaction may be a symptom of the need to invest more energy into rediscovering each other. This leveling off of excitement in your brain is a necessary phenomenon that keeps you exploring and reinventing your world. Without it you would become depressed! As a couple, you can use this knowledge to continually reinvent your relationship. Otherwise, you may go on to divorce your second and third spouse when you could have possibly reinvented the relationship with your first!

Obviously, not all relationships or marriages are meant to last. Sometimes we get married too young or the other person is not capable or motivated to improve a relationship. All relationships deserve to go through a process of honest reevaluation. I remember hearing about a well-known minister who said that he and his wife went away on their anniversary every year and answered the question of whether they wanted to "re-up" for another year. They talked about what would improve their marriage and what they would change. Then during the next year, they each took responsibility for carrying out aspects of their joint plan for the year. They also made a commitment to each other; if either felt that in spite these efforts their marriage may have run its full course, they would seek marriage counseling. That way, they would be guided to a good conclusion. They wanted their relationship to have a decent burial if that was the case! They viewed honesty as a core value in their relationship as well as seeking professional help to guide them. If I could propose a golden rule for all couples, I would recommend they commit to similar yearly evaluations, "re-ups," and new plans of action. Sadness, hopelessness, and anger are meant to be signs to take action, not to have an affair. The pain inflicted on our mates and families can be avoided when we use our leadership skills to be honest, face our fears, and develop a plan for resolution.

Many fallen leaders seem to have turned to opportunities around them for this "high." All relationships, especially those in these very public, fast-paced lifestyles, are in need of continual strengthening, reinvestment, and reevaluation. Gamblers who delight in the rush of the winnings are addicted to the feeling of the dopamine release in their brains. It is difficult to have self-awareness. Even the best gambling-addicted CEOs who run tight ships based on their profit and loss statements can rarely tell you the same overall analysis of their gambling winnings or losses for the year. They instead focus on their big winnings and seem vague about their losses. They love the excitement of the anticipation as well as the occasional winning itself, which provides a steady flow of dopamine to the brain!

If you combine the love of excitement with impaired limit-setting behaviors and an overly inflated sense of importance learned from childhood, it can be a dangerous combination. Parents of these individuals may not have set appropriate limits or held their child responsible for their behavior. They would not have been expected to cooperate with others in a respectful and reciprocal way. These children, as adults, might have a lowered ability to handle frustration or focus on long term planning.

Studies of gambling behaviors have revealed how risk-taking involving winning and losing is hard-wired into our brains. No matter how much you rationally calculate to spend ahead of time, losing money at the casino has a tendency to trigger your spending even more. Similar to losing money is "almost winning". A study published in the journal Neuron in 2009 found that almost winning activates the win-related circuitry within the brain and enhances the motivation to gamble. "Gamblers often interpret near-misses as special events, which encourage them to continue to gamble," said Luke Clark of the University of Cambridge. "Our findings show that the brain responds to near-misses as if a win has been delivered, even though the result is technically a loss." (Clark, Luke, "Gambling Near-Misses Enhance Motivation to Gamble and Recruit Win-Related Brain Circuitry" Neuron, Volume 61, Issue 3, 12 February 2009, doi:10.1016/j.neuron.2008.12.031)

The Amygdala Hijack

So far we have seen that it is a complex combination of factors that leads to poor choices. Add another factor of the normal stressful lives of leaders, and you get an even higher chance of being outed! In basic terms, brains and bodies under stress are not properly equipped for self-control. Stress activates the sympathetic nervous system—the fight, flight, or freeze response.

The term *amygdala hijack* comes from a noted author, Daniel Goleman, who wrote the popular book *Emotional Intelligence: Why It Can Matter More Than IQ*. He used this phrase to describe how with a perceived threat, the stimuli go right to your amygdala and also to your "thinking brain," the neocortex. (The prefrontal cortex is an advanced subdivision of this neocortex.) A record of experiences in your hippocampus (your memory center) looks for a match to other historically dangerous threats, finds it, and tells the amygdala that it is a fight, flight, or freeze situation.

In these situations, you can react irrationally or even destructively. The amygdala triggers the   sympathetic nervous system, hijacking the rational brain. Focused now on survival, your emotional brain can process this information milliseconds earlier than your rational brain. You will bypass the entire thinking brain. Stress leads to poor decisions. Goleman also states that "self-control is crucial . . . when facing someone who is in the throes of an 'amygdala hijack' so as to avoid a complementary hijacking whether in work situations, or in private life."

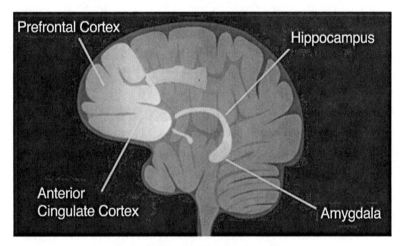

Amygdala Hijack in Review

Perceived threat goes right to your amygdala and prefrontal cortex (thinking brain). The memory center (hippocampus) searches for history in order to tell the amygdala to fight, flight or freeze.

(Brain Basics http://www.nimh.nih.gov/health/educational-resources/brainbasics/.shtml)

The Science of Willpower

Kelly McGonigal, PhD, draws from the disciplines of psychology, neuroscience, and economics in her book *The Willpower Instinct*. She states,

> Some neuroscientists go so far as to say that we have one brain but two minds—or even, two people living inside our mind. There's the version of us that acts on impulse and seeks immediate gratification, and the version of us that controls our impulses and delays gratification to protect our long-term goals. They're both of us, but we switch back and forth between these two selves. Sometimes we identify with the person who wants to lose weight, and sometimes we identify with the person who just wants the cookie. This is what defines a willpower challenge: Part of you wants one thing, and another part of you wants something else. Or your present self wants one thing, but your future self would be better off if you did something else. (The Willpower Instinct, 2012)

Even though we flip-flop between the two voices of yes and no, McGonigal says we need both. If we didn't have impulsive desires, we wouldn't pursue enjoyment; we might instead feel unmotivated or downright depressed. These two opposing parts can and do work together. If what we desire comes with a big negative such as high price tag or high danger, our more primitive instinct, our "gut reaction" can agree with our wiser self, which is already saying no. The willpowered self can only be operational if you handle your stress throughout the day.

Willpower is not simply about being true to your values; it is about ensuring your brain has plenty of sleep, good food, proper exercise, and ongoing stress reduction each day to act on those values.

The Domino Effect

A domino effect can easily happen when one poor decision is made in a distracted or unaware moment. A pathway is created before us to follow. An example would be choosing to stay up an hour past your normal bedtime to watch a TV show. The next morning, you are too tired to jump out of bed and do your morning workout at the gym. You feel grumpy all morning because you are missing your exercise high, which normally makes you feel energized and positive throughout the day. Research shows that if you are feeling bad about making a mistake, it can lead to other bad decisions. With your brain now under stress, you may say "what the heck" and order the blue plate special at lunchtime or go out for drinks after work. While you may occasionally enjoy staying up late to watch sports playoffs or the Oscars as one of life's pleasures, if you don't keep a routine that maintains your balance, you are setting yourself up for other "bad" decisions. Your brain will always default to what is easiest—impulsive satisfaction in the moment.

Avoiding Impulsivity

You have just read of the body's fight-or-flight stress response, which activates the brain's amygdala when you recognize an external threat. This focuses every bit of your physical and mental energy to respond. Energy (fat and sugar) as well as stress hormones are instantly pumped into your body so that you act and act fast. By monopolizing all the energy, your prefrontal cortex—the area of the brain in charge of impulse control, long-range goals, and willpower—is virtually shut down. Your digestive system is also shut down, and you may experience dry mouth. This is not the time to eat! Right now your body is saying, "Move! Don't stand there thinking! Danger! Get out of here!"

In order to overcome impulsivity, it is important to breathe and slow your heart rate so that you don't shut down the wisdom and willpower found in your prefrontal cortex. Reaching for self-control engages the parasympathetic nervous system to help you stay calm. You need a good heart variability, which comes from being relaxed. You need your brain to be fed energy to have the power to make good decisions. Your prefrontal cortex can then communicate the need for self-control to the lower brain regions, keeping your heart at a slower rhythm and your blood pressure normal.

It's Your Higher Self Calling!

Jack Abramoff is a former lobbyist, businessman, writer, and movie producer. He was one of the most powerful lobbyists in U.S. history and personally consulted with some of the highest profile politicians and public figures in the country. It was said that if you wanted a political favor, Jack Abramoff could get it for you, perhaps even with the White House. Then he was outed. Abramoff was convicted of bribing public officials, tax evasion, extortion, and fraud and sentenced to five years for his crimes. His fall was complete, utter, and total. His marriage ended, his rich friends left him, and politicians by the hundreds scrambled to mitigate their relationship to Mr. Abramoff; however, many public officials went down with him.

In prison, Abramoff had the opportunity to correct the flaws within his own character. Prison is a place where more than three million U.S. citizens are making amends for risky behaviors, addictions, crime, and myriad BeOUTEDtudes. Even in prisons, however, many men and women still cannot correct the character gap and return to a place of peace and ethical values. Denial covers the uncomfortable truth.

Jack Abramoff, however, took his "outing" and closed the loop. Today he attempts to work from a higher set of values. After his release, he worked in a local pizza shop for $7.50 an hour while living in a halfway house. He comments that he found genuine friendships for the first time in his life. Abramoff worked diligently on reforming his own values while attempting to expose the ugliness of Washington lobbyist efforts in his book, *Capital Punishment, the Hard Truth about Washington Corruption from America's Most Notorious Lobbyist (Nov. 2011)*. To this day, Abramoff works diligently to expose corruption and clean up lobbyist efforts.

For Abramoff, being outed was the best thing that could have happened to him. He freely admits it. His higher self knew that, and at some level he probably agreed to the shameful outing and to serve time for his offenses. He has found peace from his outing and is living without the deep character gap felt by so many who live secret lives or who succumb to addictive and risky behaviors.

Bernie Madoff fooled thousands into giving his company hundreds of millions of dollars to safely invest. He had everything money could buy—houses, yachts, cars—and enjoyed a lavish lifestyle. After his outing, however, Madoff was quoted as saying that while living in an eight-by-eight-foot cell, he had finally found some peace and was living an honest lifestyle. For some, it takes a personal tragedy.

We can change our current situations at any time. Doing so takes honesty in which we look squarely into the mirror and deal with what is staring back at us. We say to this image, "Okay, I'm not totally in love with what I see, but I can accept you. I'm not totally pleased with where I am, but I can begin to learn from past mistakes and start acting on what is better for me."

Whether it takes prison or a lesser wake-up call, I believe each person's higher self wishes to return to walking on a higher road. The good news is that now we begin to know the importance of evaluating our lives and pursuing our dreams and that which feels soul inspired. We know the importance of healing our self-worth, changing our stressful lifestyles, and making strong spiritual connections. We can begin to use the knowledge of science behind our impulsive and sometimes destructive acts to keep ourselves "in the thinking zone" to master strong willpower. In future chapters you will find a further explanation of techniques that help reduce self-sabotaging behavior. Our BeOUTEDtudes can then change to self-awareness and self-mastery, a key component of an authentic leader. The next two chapters will help you consider a course of action to take control of your life.

CHAPTER 3

The Path to Healing

Healing may not be so much about getting better, as about letting go
of everything that isn't you—all of the expectations,
all of the beliefs—and becoming who you are.
—Rachel Naomi Remen, MD

Healing the Wounds of Self-Worth

Healing starts with acceptance of where we are in our lives today. To begin, we must dig deep into what we have come to believe about ourselves and how we view the world at large. We were taught how to see the world and our place in it by beliefs from our parents, our churches, our education, and our life experiences as children. These are not all negative beliefs to be sure, for we were also endowed with many positive core beliefs as well. However, it is those implanted negative self-beliefs that we must change in our life journeys toward authentic and successful leadership. These beliefs and the resulting lack of faith in our ability to change our situations keep us from taking action to pursue our dreams. We stay too long in unhealthy, unfulfilling jobs and relationships. We approach new situations in our lives and businesses with baggage from the past. The stored-up fears, resentments, and angers can be destructive and unproductive.

Negative beliefs about ourselves come from negative conditioning and from experiencing a gamut of small to large traumas during our lifetimes. They are the root cause of most of our personal difficulties and shortcomings and therefore play a vital role in our leadership journeys. Rather than healing these negative beliefs by looking at their origins, we often mask them and hide them so others will not see our shortcomings. This is the path away from authentic leadership, not toward it. It is also the path away from living a fulfilling life. The hiding creates feelings of emptiness, depression, and anxiety. We believe consciously or unconsciously that something is wrong with us. We often want to self-medicate to fill the emptiness within us. At our disposal is a variety of euphoric-like highs. We use the "overs," and there are many: overspending, overworking, and overeating, along with drugs, drinking, gambling, Internet gaming, pornography, or relationship addictions. The "highs" we receive are only a temporary relief. They do not offer true authentic happiness, which can only come from a healthy sense of self-worth.

The negative beliefs we received came from many sources. You're bad if you don't clean your room . . . You are born sinful and must seek penance . . . You aren't important if you are not in the gifted class . . . You're not as pretty as others—the list goes on and on, and sadly we often come to believe these negative opinions of ourselves at a very young age, not even realizing we will carry them through our adult lives, sometimes with great pain and even suffering. Jerry Sandusky, the former football coach at Penn State, might easily be the villain for his crimes against young boys, yet as a young boy he was probably a victim as well and played out the scenario over and over again in his adult life. The illustration is certainly extreme, but in lesser ways, we all replay dramas from these implanted hurts and beliefs. Perhaps none of us can honestly throw the first stone at such perpetrators.

An Inside Job

This journey of self-discovery of our true worth is the most important work we will do in our lives. When we fully accept ourselves, we have more integrated personal lives, which sustain us in our leadership roles. We also possess greater faith in our own abilities, and we ignite that belief in those around us.

From a place of strength, a leader can mentor others to remove the obstacles to their own worth in both direct and indirect ways. A staff member who could not trust parental figures to be emotionally available and provide for their needs in childhood may suspect your ability to be trustworthy and present for them. In my first CEO position, I had a staff member who had unhealed issues from a very dominating father. We typically had a good relationship. On occasion, when I became a bit questioning or direct about a situation or decision she had made, she visibly reacted and accused me of being too accusatory and verbally assaultive. Emotionally, it brought her back to the hurt caused by her father.

Although I tried to work around this issue, it became more productive for me to directly ask her to question the hurt and the true source of her strong reaction to me. In time, she saw the connection and worked on it, sometimes with a humorous comment. If I had come from an unhealed place within me or taken her aggression at face value, I could have interpreted her behavior as a personal assault. Role-modeling the payoffs to inner healing work and having an understanding of our past conditioning has become a part of my leadership mentoring, all while continuing my own inner work in leadership.

We all desire to be respected, validated, and even admired. Often this desire is a motivator for why people wish to be in leadership roles. If you cannot feel respect for yourself, you cannot feel respect for others. What you long for, you cannot give; therefore, self-respect eludes you in leadership and can lead to failure. Respect is a universal desire of everyone around us. When we realize that respect begins with ourselves and does not necessarily come from others until we find it within, the impact of this revelation on leadership is profound. The leader who desires respect from others may appear emotionally needy or egocentric and garner the opposite—disrespect. It is always an inside job first!

Call Out the Thieves

When you can identify negative beliefs in your life and call them out for the thieves they have been in your journey so far, you begin to live at a higher, more positive "frequency." You will begin to tune into a higher frequency of people and opportunities. You will begin to live your life from a different, less wounded foundation. The door will open for the right relationships, friends, and jobs to come forward. The heavy burden of hiding, guilt, shame, and compromise will fall away. You will begin to sweep up past messes, toss out old furniture that has not served you well, and organize your inner rooms to your liking.

This process of healing old beliefs—that we are bad, sinful, unworthy, unlovable, and average—is easier if we are honest about needing help with these repeated reactions and patterns in our lives. Most of us have taken careful steps to hide our shame, fear, inadequacies, and guilt. We do not want to admit that we keep attracting the same kind of negative patterns in our lives. Some of us have tucked our shadow natures so deep that we aren't even aware of their daily effect on our lives.

Traumatic events are stored in our brains and our bodies unless we had a way to process them into a healthy resolution at the time. If we didn't have anyone to help us see the bigger picture, the real truth of the situation, we invariably absorbed it as a core negative belief. When we process these issues with the help of modalities that mobilize our information processing systems, we now can link the original trauma to more current positive experiences and understandings of ourselves.

I worked with a woman who simply could not lose excess weight. She complained that she had tried every diet and every drug, all without success. If she lost a few pounds on a diet, she would gain them back and more. Her health suffered, as did her relationships and lifestyle. While she wanted a leadership role, she knew in her heart she wasn't ready. Then one day, she answered an ad for weight loss through hypnosis. She went to an organizational meeting and realized it would be costly, but she held out the belief that she *had* to heal. She felt her life depended on it.

Through hypnotic therapy, the woman was reminded of a long-held negative belief that she "wouldn't amount to anything" given to her by critical parents and that "being fat ran in the family." None of this was true, of course, but she had come to believe it. Through this therapy, a different image was planted in her mind, one that ultimately convinced her that she was worthy of success and that the weight was simply a heavy negative belief she held to be true and was no longer.

The weight began to fall off her. Her countenance brightened, and her smile returned. Dress sizes fell, and new opportunities appeared all around her. One day she came into my office and told me she was engaged to be married to a wonderful man. She beamed with happiness. In the office, she became the problem solver rather than the problem employee. In short, her life completely transformed. She never regained the weight, she married the man of her dreams, and today she runs her own nonprofit agency. How did this happen? She was able to reprogram a deep-seated false belief about herself.

Self-Worth Is Leader Work!

While the work is yours to do, help is all around us. Try to be honest with yourself about the degree and kind of healing you wish to master as you read examples in this and other chapters. At times leaders shy away from the healing journey because of past misperceptions that receiving help, including psychotherapy or counseling of any kind, means we are weak or mentally ill. In truth, embarking on a healing process means the exact opposite. I have found it to be a courageous piece of work, eye-opening, highly supportive, and absolutely life enhancing.

I enjoy not reacting to my "triggered hot spots" in the same way or to the degree I did before! I enjoy living inside my own body, mind, and spirit now and the level of freedom healing has given me. I am not at the mercy of my past. I am in control and directing my future! The results can be dramatic, even life changing. This is personal alchemy, permanent change, transforming base lead into gold . . . feeling alive!

So, let's get down and personal! I would like to offer some examples of core negative beliefs often held in different areas of our lives. I encourage you to take time, make notes, sit with your true higher nature, and access your deepest negative beliefs that might be keeping you from your greatest success.

Core Negative Beliefs

Basic core negative beliefs are beliefs we hold to be true about ourselves. They are usually created when we are children but can also be created during traumatic or significant times in our adult lives. The following are examples of commonly held beliefs contributed by Sharon from her work with clients and her study of various psychotherapy modalities:

- **I'm not good enough**—I am clumsy, I am worthless, I am unsuccessful, I am not very talented, I can't succeed, I am stupid, I am inadequate.
- **I'm not loveable**—I am not special, I'm not worthy, I don't matter, I don't deserve love, I deserve only bad things.
- **I'm at fault or responsible**—I'm to blame, I should have done something, I should have known better, I cannot trust my judgment, I deserve to die, I did something wrong, I have to be perfect.
- **I am unwanted**—I am alone, I don't fit in, I am unimportant, I don't belong.
- **I am defective**—I am bad, I am fat, I will fail, I don't deserve love, I am ugly, I am not beautiful enough, I am permanently damaged.
- **I am powerless**—I'm not safe, I am a victim, I am afraid, I am helpless, I cannot protect myself, I am vulnerable, I'll never be able to do it, I can't say no, I am

powerless, I cannot get what I want, I'm not in control, I cannot trust.

- **I'm not competent**—I'll get it wrong, I can't understand, I'm not understood, I don't know what to do, I can't trust myself.
- **I can't make a commitment**—I need to meet my needs first, I can't be responsible for others.
- **I'm more important**—I have rights and privileges that come with my importance, I am entitled to do what I want to do regardless of the cost, I refuse to exercise control when it comes to my impulses.

Suspect Our Core Beliefs First—Then Do a "Rewind"

We may be aware of these beliefs and others within ourselves, but some of them are difficult to access consciously, much less heal. We often react without really knowing the inner negative belief at the core of our feelings or actions. When beliefs are positive, they provide a solid foundation that serves to affirm and support us throughout life. For instance, a core belief that has convinced us that we are smart or able to deal well with challenges provides self-confidence and energy for taking initiative. Conversely, the negative and self-limiting programming creates obstacles for us.

A good habit to develop is one of "suspecting our core beliefs first." Whenever we find ourselves having painful or negative feelings, we begin by asking ourselves what we are feeling and what we are telling ourselves. We learn that most of our uncomfortable feelings are self-created—not externally caused. This means we must let go of the idea that outside people or events "make us" feel. Giving up the victim notion that others are in charge of our feelings is the first step that leads us to address and heal core negative beliefs.

The good news is that we can learn to recognize when those negative beliefs are "running our lives" and become more and more adept at dissipating their negative impact. By becoming conscious of them, we can learn to discern what triggers them. When we grow overreactive (fearful, angry, confused, jealous, or upset) at a situation, this may be a sign that a negative self-belief has been triggered.

First, we can question the overreaction. When we have a calm moment, we can reflect on the situation and experience the feelings, bodily reactions, and negative beliefs that were activated. One exercise that is common practice in psychotherapy is to rewind our life movie back to a similar scene from childhood or an earlier time. In EMDR (eye movement desensitization and reprocessing therapy), a similar technique is called *float-back*. By witnessing past trauma for the present emotion, we can be empathetic to our current situation and perhaps reduce the "charge." It is often healing to witness what circumstance created the feeling in the first place. For significant trauma, you may choose to utilize a therapeutic intervention like EMDR, which can help you desensitize and reprocess these triggers. We will discuss EMDR and other tools in chapter 5.

We feel a freedom previously unknown when we take steps to heal these wounds completely and replace them with positive beliefs about ourselves, just as the example of the young woman who suffered from excess weight.

Our negative beliefs can control our day-to-day decisions, lead to unethical behavior, and destroy the trust others put in us. The person or company that harbors no secrets is an individual or company that thrives because the foundation is strong and can withstand many challenges. We need a solid foundation in order to lead with the alchemy of true self-esteem, not overcompensation or grandiosity.

Let's look at an example of a typical philosophical negative belief. John has been waiting for an opportunity for advancement at his nonprofit organization. His vice president retired, and the executive director is interviewing two internal candidates and two external candidates to replace the retiring vice president. John is one of the internal candidates. He has worked hard for several years. He has been a loyal and valuable team player.

Because John grew up with three very talented brothers, all older than him, John always believed he wasn't as good as his older brothers in sports and academics. This led to a life of underachievement and timidity that worked on John's behalf in his role as a team player but against his personality as a leader. He held a belief about himself that he wasn't as talented as those around him. John didn't get the promotion, and the agency brought in an outside candidate for the job. John was angry and rationalized to himself that the agency was unfair and didn't support or appreciate him. This feeling was a core belief John had adopted because of the intense competition with his brothers. They were unfair to him, didn't support him, and didn't appreciate him. John was unsupportive of the new hire and quickly fell out of favor with the new vice president, leading eventually to his resignation.

Do you understand the negative core belief John held about himself and the resulting set of circumstances he created? Our habit is to place blame for our feelings. I'm not implying John didn't deserve the promotion. I am saying, however, that the hired vice president did not create John's feelings; John did. To be able to make this distinction removes us from living life blown about like leaves in the wind.

Let's look at another example. Perhaps you felt unappreciated by your busy parents. Perhaps you had a mother or father who didn't share her or his love in an endearing way. Can you begin to see how a deep unhealed negative belief that you are unappreciated could affect your adult relationships? Can you notice how a somewhat distant boss who doesn't overtly recognize your talent and worth to the company might trigger that negative belief you hold about yourself or how a cool, somewhat uncaring mate in life might trigger your feelings of being unlovable or unappreciated?

Every one of us can recall driving to work and someone coming into our traffic lane and almost hitting us. Several unhealed negative beliefs might be triggered in this situation: *I'm unsafe, I'm not respected, I'm not important!* When the shock and audacity of the driver hits you and you first feel angry, you have some choices. You can react to the anger by blasting him or her with your horn, or you can become instantly aware of the anger, count to five, and replace it with gratitude that the driver didn't hit you! In an instant, you can convert anger and rage to a deep feeling of gratitude that you are safe and unhurt.

Here are some affirmations you might use in this situation:

- I am okay. I am glad I was alert.
- I am safe. I was being protected by seeing that one!
- The monkey on his or her shoulder doesn't have to jump into my car.
- Hope your day gets better, because you are not ruining mine!

How we react and process when provoked is the key. How we respond from that inner dialogue in a conscious, aware state of mind is the game changer. When we understand that we are in total charge of our feelings, we move to a whole new level of mastery over life. By analyzing our reactions, we are then free to choose how we are going to feel and respond. Our happiness is no longer dictated by someone else's words or behavior. We are no longer victims. There is no outside influence that controls our feelings. Even if the external circumstances can trigger emotional responses, we still have a say in how we ultimately express those responses and what influence those responses will have on our lives.

What Triggered You?

When you feel pain, anger, sadness, or depressive thoughts, stop and consciously take three deep breaths. What nettled you? Was it the driver cutting you off in traffic? Was it someone pointing toward you on the street? Was it a friend who didn't call you back? Was it a moment of sadness when you heard a song? When the emotion enters your consciousness, stop, breathe deeply again, and ask yourself that important question: what possible negative belief did this elicit for me to heal?

If you can avoid reacting to the negative emotion and instead question the feeling of it first, you cut the negative loop cycle. You haven't healed the wound, but you have slowed the insidious pattern of unconsciously reacting to it. Depending on the nature and depth of the unhealed negative belief, you may be able to dissipate the emotion with attention and empathy to its origins. If not, I have provided effective healing techniques in chapter 5.

Negative Relationship Patterns in Life

In addition to negative beliefs, psychologists have defined common negative relationship patterns that develop early in life. Called a schema, it is a strongly held positive or negative belief that a person believes not only about him—or herself but also about other people or the world in general. Whole populations of people can hold schemas as well. Prejudice and even genocide are examples. A person's life may reveal a pattern of difficulty caused by these negative beliefs. The theme of these problems often remains the same over time and repeats itself in different types of relationships, including romantic involvements, business relationships, and friendships.

If we maintain a constant negative opinion of events unfolding in our lives, such as the inevitability of a failing nation, failing politics, a failing company, failing health, etc., even the most positive relationship will be impossible to maintain unless we surround ourselves with others of the same negative core schema.

Most often, negative schemas develop at an early age. If not healed, they continue to be harmful to a person's self-esteem and relationships. I gave a description of a typical family of origin of someone who acts out in an entitled or grandiose way in an earlier chapter, citing a childhood deficient in internal limits and responsibility to others. Psychologist Jeffrey Young, a leading researcher on schemas, has defined eleven of the most common life traps (schemas) that develop early in life. You can read the book *Reinventing Your Life* (Young, J.E. & Klosko, J.S., May 1, 1994) or go to www.schematherapy.com to view a comprehensive list of these schemas.

My Own Schemas

As an exercise to see the impact of life's traumas upon your beliefs about yourself, others, the world around you, and the trauma itself, choose a relatively small to medium trauma that has happened to you, perhaps when you were younger. You may want to explore a trauma in your parents' or grandparents' history and evaluate how the negative life schemas were passed down to you.

My trauma is _____.

Now please respond to the following questions about the result of this trauma:

- What belief do you hold about yourself? (I am inferior, I'm bad for letting it happen, etc.)
- What belief do you hold about others? (I'm all alone, No one cares or one can be trusted, etc.)
- What belief do you have about the world and the future? (The world is a dangerous place, etc.)
- What belief do you have about the trauma? (Harm is random, I'll never be able to heal, etc.)

Negative schemas can affect our leadership journeys. If we hold pessimistic views of ourselves and our place in the world, what type of leaders do our employees and stakeholders see? If we hold strong fear of abandonment based upon some unhealed childhood experience, what happens when our best employee decides to leave the company for a better job?

If we have a negative schema that drives us to constantly seek approval, how difficult will it be to discipline an employee or fire him? What type of executive would you be if you constantly sought recognition for yourself because of a deep need to be recognized?

In the next chapter, we will review common negative beliefs in the various "rooms" of your home and provide exercises to change these beliefs. No one has the power to keep you from the success you desire and that is rightfully yours. It is possible to set your sights on your goal; heal any blockage from negative beliefs; mobilize your visual, mental, and emotional energy; and confidently know the results are already on their way to you!

You can shift the accelerator into high gear and begin to taxi down the leadership runway until . . . with a gentle lift of your intention you nose upward and soon are soaring high above everyone around you. This is the "leadership lift," and it soon separates you from others who couldn't or wouldn't do the necessary healing. No one except you keeps you from success—*no one.*

CHAPTER
4

Meeting Your Leader on the Road

Life isn't about finding yourself.
It's about creating yourself.
—George Bernard Shaw

We hunt for meaning and seek answers to life's complex issues. We endeavor to make something of our lives. Yet we often don't feel truly happy. As stated in chapter 3, we look in strange places for happiness: extreme sports, overachievement, and the long list of "overs"— spending, eating, drugs, drinking, gambling, working, etc. We find that these solutions truly work! For the moment, we can't be in deep angst if we are eating chocolate cake or having a cocktail. Yet these short-term repeat solutions have all sorts of negative consequences. We know we need another answer.

Perhaps the words written in the Bible provided the answer: "Knock and the door will open. Ask and it will be given to you." We don't need to look any further for the answer to wholeness than within ourselves. If we could magically peel the onion layers back from our deep negative inner beliefs right to the core of our essence, we would probably find joy waiting for us. More than likely, we would find our wise, loving, and tender higher selves patiently waiting to welcome us home.

The Bible also taught that the "kingdom of heaven is within." Once we heal even a single layer of negativity from ourselves, we get close enough to sip from the sweetness of a new reality within and around us. Perhaps the kingdom of happiness and fulfillment is somewhere within us rather than somewhere out there.

The world changes as our reality changes, and for better or worse, whatever image we hold within ourselves is similar to how the world appears to us. Steven Tyler of the rock group Aerosmith recently talked with Oprah Winfrey about transformation. He said, "You can only change yourself, but when you do, isn't it funny how everybody around you changes too?"

Flushing Out the Truth

When you read the BeOUTEDtudes, you saw the vulnerability of leaders who held those attitudes. The good and perhaps bad news is that in leadership positions, it is difficult to hide. Our instant social media networks can give the world a firsthand account of any coping behavior that is not in keeping with our public servant images.

As the people in the world evolve their standards as a whole, perhaps this energetically pushes all the negativity to the surface, much like Mother Nature cleansing Earth by erupting into volcanoes, floods, hurricanes, and tornadoes. We can no longer run from ourselves or others, as everything is being flushed to the surface. You can be sure that anything less than the truth will be revealed to us—and perhaps to everyone around us as well.

It is important to remember that we are not going backward when we face these areas of our lives; we are going inward. It is only in that inner sanctuary that we have the power to locate and heal anything that is not life enhancing. There is no other way to go but through this process if you want to be an authentic leader. We all know that there are plenty of inauthentic ones. Healing and releasing ourselves from the wounds of childhood means that we come back into that congruency. We are not living life crippled by past repetitive dramas.

Your Assignment Is . . .

My wife, Sharon, has held many hands and hearts over her thirty-eight years as a psychotherapist and later as a certified professional coach and interfaith minister. She holds the view that in addition to a life calling or purpose, each person has the important mission of transforming the negative core beliefs gained from his or her experiences. The healing that is done on these beliefs is unique to each of us. When we heal these beliefs, we are freed to live out our potential, and our transformed selves become great gifts to humanity.

Never underestimate the contribution made by healing one small negative belief about yourself. When anyone, especially leaders, heal, it has a ripple effect on others. The peaceful vibration of someone who has released the pain, corrected negative beliefs, and accepted his or her worth is energetically felt by everyone around him or her. In that leader's presence, one can feel personal integrity and inner peace.

The new positive beliefs, the new way of viewing ourselves and the world are contributed to the mass consciousness, and we all evolve. In short, all people have an earthly assignment to return to the truth of who they are.

Becoming congruent with who you truly are is the most precious gift you can give yourself. It also is the most powerful form of alchemy in the world. After releasing the negative, we are left with wholeness, a powerful magnet drawing what we desire. We have gleaned the valuable learning and claimed the strength that resulted. Our very cells are aligned in a congruency of body, mind, and spirit. We own our lives and are at the helm of our leadership positions. From our own evolution, we can better maximize our contribution to the world.

Believing!

Unlike the "enlightenment" of the Christian apostle Paul on the road to Damascus or the sudden nirvana of Siddhartha into the Buddha beneath the banyan tree, our awakening is usually far more gradual, and we often need wake-up calls before we do our inner work. Bill (who never used his last name), the founder of Alcoholics Anonymous, summed it up pretty well: "I got sick and tired of feeling sick and tired."

For many of us, regretfully our journeys begin in similar places:

- I'm tired of living in debt. I'll never get this turned around.
- I'm sick of being overweight. There is no hope I'll ever be thin again.
- I can't take this dead-end job another week. I should just resign myself to it.

- I'm miserable living alone. There is no one out there for me.
- I'm exhausted being a seeker. There is nothing to find, nothing to discover.
- Work, work, work! Kill me now!

When we begin to believe the nevers, the nothings, the no hopes, the kill me nows, we have come to believe the great lie—that change cannot happen for us. When believing stops, life begins to cease as well. Sickness and disease are often right around the corner. When we cease to believe, the body will find a way to stop as well. The correlation between pessimistic thought and the natural health of our bodies has been well documented.

A Knock on the Door

Every negative thought also can contain the seeds for change:

- I'm tired of living in debt. *There must be a better way.*
- I'm sick of being overweight. *Something must work.*
- I can't take this dead-end job another week. *There must be something else.*
- I'm miserable living alone. *How can I find a meaningful relationship?*
- I'm exhausted being a seeker. *I need to be a finder.*
- Work, work, work! *Where is the joy in living?*

Do any of these scenarios sound remotely familiar? Read them again. They are not just negative statements, for they end with another statement, a knock on the door:

- *There must be a better way!*
- *Something must work!*
- *There must be something else!*
- *How can I find a meaningful relationship?*
- *I need to be a finder!*
- *Where is the joy in living?*

As long as we long for change in our lives, there is hope. *Believing* is the key component to change. It takes really wanting to change. Wanting something different means we are "sick and tired of being sick and tired."

Repeat Performances

The all-important first step to healing any negative belief about ourselves is to become aware of that belief. You might not have been aware of why you act the way you do in relationships, but clearly there are reasons when you examine them closely. Have you seen repeated behaviors, repeated attraction to certain kinds of relationships, or repeated coping methods? Do you have negative self-talk?

Examine this list of negative beliefs and make a list of those that apply:

> I don't deserve (love, good things happening, etc.).
> I am afraid of being alone.
> I cannot trust myself.
> I cannot succeed.
> I will fail.
> I am not in control.
> I have to be perfect to please others.

I am powerless.

I am unimportant.

I am a bad person.

I cannot get what I want.

I am inadequate.

I am shameful.

I am unimportant.

I am a disappointment.

I did something wrong.

I do not deserve.

I cannot succeed.

I am not lovable.

As you examine this list, answer the following questions:

- Is there a specific memory or memories where this belief originated?
- In your leadership position, how does this negative belief show itself?
- Do any areas of your life's hot spots trigger this negative belief?
- Are there any negative beliefs you have that were not listed?

For Every Problem There Is a Solution

Once you've identified possible negative relationship beliefs, get moving on them. Remember that in nature, for every "problem" (e.g., poison ivy) there is also a solution (e.g., jewelweed) growing right alongside it. I believe that, just as in business, if there is a problem, there is also a solution close by.

Make self-forgiveness a daily practice. No matter what your behavior, you were not the cause of the negative core belief embedded within you. Your behavior is different from you the person. Your behavior might be labeled *bad*, but you are not a bad person. A minister friend of mine once said, "God forgives us before we ever commit errors. No matter how bad our actions, we can never be outside of God's love. God sees all acts of harm to others as simply coming from fear and disconnect from the truth of who we truly are." In the next chapter, we will discuss techniques that will directly help you release these behaviors.

Negative Beliefs and Our Inner Rooms

Let's revisit some of the inner rooms that are often the most neglected. We'll take a look at spirituality, money and finances, and family and relationships. We'll discuss some common, almost universal, negative beliefs that you might encounter in these areas and give you some exercises to heal them. You can use the ideas provided to look at the negative beliefs you may hold in other rooms in your house as well.

Spirituality and Philosophy

We begin here for a very important reason. Without a philosophy to live by, life's journey can become aimless. Many of us adopt the philosophy and beliefs of our parents. As we go forward, we become more discerning as to what parts of their belief systems fit us. Entire generations of people can carry philosophies that conflict with the beliefs of the next or former generation's philosophy. We may be left with uncertainty or even guilt for not believing as the masses do.

Some of our most endearing and beloved opinions of ourselves come from the meaningful philosophies given to us by our parents. Conversely, many of the most damning negative beliefs we come to believe about ourselves can come from them as well. These beliefs about ourselves are foundational. They give us an understanding of our innate goodness (or badness), an understanding of our inner power (or lack of it), and our relationship to a higher power, a divine self, a force of goodness and/or the presence of evil forces.

While the world holds many different philosophies and religions, history has shown that we are not terribly tolerant of the beliefs of others. Sadly, this intolerance has created wounds in all of us and been the cause of war and brutality throughout history. Becoming aware of how the negative beliefs learned throughout our lives have created roadblocks in our leadership frees us to embrace a kinder philosophy toward ourselves and the world.

Upon this Rock of Beliefs . . .

I grew up in a church environment that held individuals as innately bad and sinful. Even the liturgy expressed that statement, and it was repeated as a core belief. To be good, we needed to confess our wickedness, repent of our errant ways, and vow to be better only through divine help. When I first began to understand what those words meant, it was already too late. I tried to live as wholesome a life as I could as a teenager; however, I had common immoral thoughts at times, setting up a cycle of shame and guilt about not being a better person.

As I grew older, I gradually replaced the idea that I was inherently evil and began to question the deep-seated belief that had been part of my traditional religious upbringing. Instead of the shame, failure, and guilt about pledging to live a better life, I gradually realized that there wasn't anything inherently wrong with me as I had been told. I wasn't rotten to the core of my being. It took years for me to overcome that liturgical belief: By nature, you are sinful and unclean.

Think of the core beliefs you hold from your childhood religious experiences. Place them squarely in front of you. Many religions did not teach us to honor our own divine nature. Once we recognize these limiting beliefs, we can cognitively begin to counter them through building our own spiritual philosophy. We recognize that it was based on a fundamental untruth from an unhealed parent or philosophical belief that may have been originated by human beings to control others instead of supporting their expansion.

As we begin to replace the negative beliefs with more positive belief statements, our core reality begins to shift. We learn that maybe there is nothing wrong with us at our core! We are capable of being loved and loving someone else from this new view. This is the alchemical transformation that takes us from feeling inherently bad and alone to becoming confident and connected to everyone and everything. This is the journey back to wholeness—dropping long-held negative beliefs and replacing them with reinforcing positive ones.

Money and Finances

Negative money beliefs are not mere fleeting thoughts. They run a hidden program much like software, sabotaging your best intents. They are the small "voices" in your head that actually override what you'd like to believe but don't. What goes on in your subconscious wields much more power than your conscious mind.

Behaviorists have estimated that more than 90 percent of mental activities take place subconsciously. As a child you may have heard your parents arguing or discussing financial issues. You may have heard that your family was poor or struggling to pay the bills. You may have felt their fear and grew afraid yourself.

For most of us, negative beliefs about money were embedded in our subconscious as children. For those who grew up extremely poor, the negative belief was deeply embedded, perhaps even creating a dominant lifelong energy to never be poor again.

I once asked a good friend of mine why he lived in such a huge home in the suburbs of Washington, D.C., a home many might call an estate or a mansion. He and his wife were the only occupants of the house, and they loved to entertain guests. When I asked him, he thought pensively for a moment and then described the house he had grown up in as a boy.

He described it meticulously: pine boards covered with tar paper, two rooms total. He, his brothers, and his parents all slept in one small room. The kitchen and living area was in the other room. They had no electricity and used kerosene lamps and candles for light and a wood-burning potbellied stove for heat and cooking. He remembered passing the biggest house in town as he walked to school and wishing it was his. I didn't need to wonder any more why he lived in that beautiful home with rooms "just to walk into and look at."

Common Negative Beliefs About Money

Listed below are beliefs about money that come from what others say. You may recognize some of them from conversations in your childhood home:

- Money is in short supply.
- It's hard to hold onto money.
- A depression can come at any moment.
- Money only comes from hard work.
- Rich people are greedy and dishonest.
- Spiritual people are not supposed to be rich.
- Rich people are seldom happy.
- There is a limit to how much I can earn.
- You could lose everything at a moment's notice.
- Money goes out faster than it comes in.

These negative money beliefs absorbed from others and combined with our personal beliefs about money are deadly combinations.

Personal Negative Beliefs About Money

- I am not good enough to make money.
- I don't deserve money or success.
- Everyone else has to come first.
- I am too stupid to make money.
- I buy for others, but it's hard to spend on myself.
- I will never be wealthy.
- I am afraid of responsibility.
- God supports others, not me.

- Miracles never happen to me.
- I am only worth minimum wage.
- I am not safe having money.
- I am no better than my parents and can't make more money than them.

How many of them do you believe? Because they often reside in our subconscious minds, we find it difficult to even recognize the negative beliefs we hold to be true. The impact they can have on our lives can be dramatic. As a successful adult, my friend who grew up in a tar-papered shack chose to have the biggest house on the block, even larger than the one that had impressed him as he walked to school as a child. Rich and successful people had big houses. The impact of that negative belief about the size and shape of a house and its relation to outward signs of success was of great importance to him.

Resources That Challenge These Beliefs

In recent years, much has been written about wealth and abundance. Napoleon Hill penned a book that has sold 20 million copies: *Think and Grow Rich*. The book was inspired by a suggestion from a Scottish-American businessman named Andrew Carnegie. While the title implies that the book deals only with how to achieve monetary wealth, the author explains that his philosophy can be used to help individuals succeed in all lines of work and to do or be almost anything they want in this world.

Other significant works followed Napoleon Hill's work, but few have had the significance of Esther and Jerry Hicks's work on the law of attraction. The law of attraction was not created by the Hicks', however. The belief that we attract what we think about and feel for was actually first posited by William Walker Atkinson in his book *Thought Vibration or the Law of Attraction in the Thought World* (1906). Many thought the work to be heretical at the time of publication, but thousands quietly read it.

Atkinson, Hill, and the Hickses wrote that humans are creators who create their own realities by their thoughts. If negative beliefs were held to be true subconsciously, the external counterpart of that negative belief would ultimately manifest itself for them.

For example, if you subconsciously believed that rich people could never be happy, wealth would not be your pursuit if you wanted a happy life. If money was the root of all evil as you might have grown up believing, your actions, consciously or not, would be to repel money from you like you would repel negative thoughts or evil people.

Can you see the effect of negative money beliefs in your life? Becoming aware of those beliefs is the first step—awareness of what we really hold to be true about money—and a primary and important assessment if we are ever to release the negative beliefs and begin to reshape our thinking.

Why is it such a big step for us to think that we can have all the wealth we desire? Is wealth really the root of all evil? Why then did the millions we raised for natural disasters in Haiti or Japan or for Hurricane Sandy along the East Coast contribute to such powerful good? Acts of kindness go on every day in every city of the world—one person giving to another with an open heart. So how can this be the root of anything but generosity and goodness?

Money is energy, an agreement that colored pieces of paper are valued at certain amounts. We consider gold to be precious, yet why is it more valuable than a chunk of granite or shale? Money is an energy medium in which we agree to the value in order to buy goods. If you hold negative opinions about money, or your worthiness to attract money, how can it flow to you? Examine your deep subconscious beliefs about money. Those thoughts will have already been manifested in your life. Correct the thought or belief, and your external life will make the correction as well.

Atkinson, and the law of attraction writers who followed him, had many interesting positions, but they all shared the following beliefs:

- The basis of life is freedom; the purpose of life is joy.
- People are creators; they create with their thoughts and emotions.
- Whatever you can imagine is yours to be, do, or have.
- The Universe or Creator wants to provide abundance; it knows your deepest desires.
- Life is not meant to be a struggle.
- You "allow" abundance starting with embracing yourself unconditionally.
- You are a child of God and have the birthright to abundance, protection, and love.

An "Abundance" of Resources!

There is a plethora of books, CDs, and websites on how to create abundance. Pick up a copy of *Think and Grow Rich*. Google the words *abundance thinking* and you will find hundreds of websites, books, and materials to help you out of the morass of negative self-beliefs about money and prosperity. This isn't some small New Age phenomenon. Thousands of books are being published on attracting abundance and wealth into your life.

Judy Goss, Suze Orman, and Manisha Thakor are well-known experts and have an abundance of books, blogs, and information to help you. Kimberly Palmer writes the Alpha Consumer blog for *US News & World Reports*, providing thoughtful insights on saving money, financial scams, debt management, and shopping smart. Her fraud and scams coverage is particularly helpful, and she publishes interesting personal finance podcasts.

There is an online radio show called <u>www.hayhouseradio.com</u>, which is an outstanding lineup of some of the top motivational coaches, psychotherapists, holistic healers, and intuitive teachers in the world. You can call in live with your questions or listen to their archives when you have time. In these shows you can find information on all areas of self-empowerment. Many of these programs provide techniques to heal your self-esteem and self-sabotage issues. They can reset your internal negative programming.

Take the time to learn solid and positive financial principles. As a leader, it will be your primary responsibility to manage the agency's cash, investments, debt, and property. If your personal financial house is not in order, it is time to get serious about cleaning and strengthening it. Too many public leaders have fallen because of greed and other fiscal misdeeds. A weak personal fiscal house is no match for the power and temptation that executive leadership brings with the job.

Time for Your $$ Inventory!

Has it been difficult to save money, to earn what you desire, or to accumulate abundance? Then it is likely that you hold core negative beliefs about money. They are so prevalent that it would be almost impossible not to hold them, and they in turn bind you. Take a moment and record what you truly believe about money. Do you believe you can be wealthy? Do you feel worthy enough to be rich? Do you believe money is tied to evil? Any answer is valid.

Now study your list. Do these beliefs really hold validity? Are they your values or your parents' or grandparents' values? What is triggered in you when you hear of an already wealthy person winning the lottery? How do you feel when a fellow coworker or CEO gets a raise and you do not? Our level of prosperous thinking can be evaluated at times like those.

Thoughts are Focused Energy! Use Them Wisely!

Becoming aware of your negative money beliefs sets you on the path to changing your financial status as well! One phrase that has been highly successful for me is to remember that *thoughts are focused energy!* What we think isn't just an insignificant internal process. Our thoughts actually are sent out all around us as energy, sometimes very powerful energy.

Animals can sense our thinking, as can aware people, especially children. Think of thoughts as energy that you are producing and sending forth. If you send negative thoughts, can you expect positive ones to be returned? But if you send thoughts of gratitude for what you do have and take steps to spend according to what is balanced for your budget, this peaceful and coherent energy is transmitted and received back to you.

If you doubt this can be true, try this experiment. Send out loving thoughts to your mate. Add loving words, even a hug or embrace. What is returned to you? Anger and a negative thought? (Well, don't interrupt someone watching their favorite television show in this exercise.) No, what is usually returned is an embrace, loving words, and reciprocated appreciation. The same holds true for abundance thinking. Thoughts are things!

Family and Relationships

The ability to love and be loved is a fundamental need of all humans. Yet many of us struggle with relationships. Most of us have failed at remaining in at least one relationship to which we committed. Loving relationships appear difficult to find, and it's harder still to maintain intimacy if you do not already have a healthy relationship with yourself. If a relationship has fulfilled its purpose and is best ended, it is possible to do so without either person being a victim or a cad. Most relationships fail without the couples healing their own negative beliefs, their own fears of intimacy and trust. Those relationships normally end in pain, hurt, and economic loss.

Harville Hendrix, founder of Imago Couple's Therapy, wrote "An Introduction to Imago" on his website (www. getting theloveyouwant.com May 2013),

> Our unconscious need is to have our feelings of aliveness and wholeness restored by someone who reminds us of our caretakers. In other words, we look for someone with the same deficits of care and attention that hurt us in the first place. So when we fall in love, when bells ring and the world seems altogether a better place, our old brain is telling us that we've

found someone with whom we can finally get our needs met. Unfortunately, since we don't understand what's going on, we're shocked when the awful truth of our beloved surfaces and our first impulse is to run screaming in the opposite direction.

How many of us have approached our most intimate relationships with the agenda that someone will now make up for all past wrongs instead of deciding to master this love within our own selves first?

Repeat Performances

The theme of these relationship problems often remains the same and repeats itself in different types of relationships, including romantic involvements, business relationships, and friendships. This is important for leaders to understand. For example, if you believe one gender or race to be fundamentally more entitled than another, look out as you take on your first executive leadership position! Clearly, not everyone holds the same core belief as you.

Generations of family conditioning, beliefs, and habits are passed down in these broad and sweeping core beliefs. Like sponges, we absorb attitudes and model our parents' behaviors. They formulate themselves into storylines that we own as definitions of who we perceive ourselves to be. If we were told by our fathers, "You'll never amount to anything," we might choose to believe we will never amount to anything and shuffle through life from job to job and relationship to relationship because we believe that negative core statement we often heard as a child.

Most of us had "good enough" parenting. However, even good enough parents have their moments of negative interaction with their children. An experience of being unappreciated and made to feel worthless can affect your adult relationships. If it was a pattern in your childhood, it will become a pattern in your adulthood and your leadership. We can even take on our parents' tones, their words, and their behaviors energetically.

An Exercise in Self-Care

Because you have hardwired and oft-rehearsed dramas from family, it is important to maintain distance from anyone who blames or in any way disrespects you on a consistent basis. Grasping the concept that your parents are passing down behavior from their caretakers helps you change your reactive behavior to a better response.

In short, see the bigger picture of how those who wounded you were also wounded. They were undoubtedly unskilled and ill prepared by their childhoods. Forgiveness may not happen overnight. Remember, forgiveness is for *you*, not for them. You deserve to release the past pain and live in the present. Accept the past by acknowledging how much you have deepened your own capacities for truth, self-awareness, and self-love. Focus on positive outcomes, make healthy choices, and allow goodness into your life in all ways possible.

Reaching Out for Help in All the Right Places

Many of us are only slightly aware of why we are depressed, angry, overweight, or unable to secure an uplifting and creative life in all of the rooms in our houses. Over time, we become disillusioned. When life's calamities strike—the death of a loved one, a failure, a career layoff, or an unexpected divorce—professional therapy is often needed to bridge the gap between pain and recovery. Women seem to support the use of therapy more than men, which is unfortunate because men need these vital services just as much as women, if not more.

Psychotherapists are trained to not only explore the negative beliefs we hold about ourselves but to help us actually release and replace them with positive ones. Some forms of depression are as life-threatening as a bout of cancer, yet some individuals who wouldn't hesitate to get medical support would avoid therapy. It's time to recognize the vital importance of our mental and emotional health and the professionals who dedicate their lives to the treatment and support of others.

Chapter 5 begins an examination of tools you can use to change and transform these nagging negative beliefs that keep you from your wholeness and your position of leadership. We are meant to live from our wholeness. The leaders within us will meet us on the road of our journeys, just as your higher self will meet you at the doorstep of your ideal inner home. The exciting and heartening fact is that there are many extremely effective self-help and professional tools that have been developed as recently as the last decade.

CHAPTER 5

Healing into Wholeness
By Sharon Massoth, LCSW

*Adverse appearances work for my good, for God utilizes every person
and every situation to bring to me my heart's desire.*
—Florence Scovil Shinn

Who Is Sitting on Your Board of Directors?

As a psychotherapist and personal life coach, I work with business leaders to change risky behaviors that threaten to sabotage their success. Leaders often consult me right before, during, or after a personal or business crisis. No matter what the crisis, I have noticed that these leaders often make self-sabotaging decisions from a much younger mind-set than their actual age. It is shocking to see how a strong leader can allow this "younger self" make executive-level decisions as if he or she were sitting on the leader's personal "board of directors." The age of the leader's younger self is often at the age when he or she was most traumatized, emotionally or physically, sometimes as young as five or six! The following are some examples.

A Fear of Separation

Donald was born to a wealthy entrepreneurial couple who became so successful that both parents often traveled internationally together. He was raised by nannies during these extended trips. He experienced the rotation and loss of many "nanny parents" over the years. He was expected not to have feelings about these losses and to "be the little man." From the age of twelve, he was sent to private boarding schools away from home. His parents doted on his accomplishments but never on *him*. Furthermore, in the culture of the '50s and '60s, his dad, a charismatic business leader, had multiple affairs, which Donald heard about or witnessed.

Donald developed wounds in the first two stages of development—the attachment stage, where you need to have a reliable source of love and comfort, and the exploration stage, where you need to be able to explore your environment from a place of support and safety. In his marriage, he was often fearful of his wife being unreliable or abandoning him. He smothered his wife with gifts and trips and kept her close by involving her in his business.

His management team reacted to the lack of boundaries and her "meddling" in their business decisions. Their respect for him as a leader diminished. When she tried to engage more fully in her own home decorating business, he found ways to sabotage it. He would repeatedly call her throughout the day for fear she was meeting new people and could have an affair. As his wife's dissatisfaction grew in this controlling relationship, she threatened to leave him. He finally agreed to receive relationship counseling.

In their counseling, she grew more compassionate toward him as she gained a clearer understanding of the etiology for his behavior. Through trial and error, they were able to develop a healthy balance of dependence and independence. Donald really understood the need for clear boundaries with his personal life at work, and the greater gift was how both he and his wife began to heal unresolved schemas from their childhoods.

A Fear of Dying

Another CEO, Patricia was part owner of a highly successful multimillion-dollar family food business where she used her natural intuition to the great advantage of her company's expansion. She came to me because of her pattern of developing anxiety about any physical illness she had, even if it was as common as a sore throat. At the very least, she was distracted from her work, and at the very worst these anxieties developed into incapacitating full-blown panic attacks during which she felt she might die.

Patricia initially was totally oblivious as to the etiology of her anxiety until we used a psychotherapy modality called EMDR (eye movement desensitization and reprocessing therapy) described later in this chapter. Using a technique called the float-back technique, she recalled a time at the age of six when she went on a two-week family vacation in Cape Cod, Massachusetts. Her family had to leave four days early because her younger three-year-old sister developed a headache and fever and was delirious, and her parents wanted to bring her back to their own pediatrician. She remembered cuddling with her sister in the backseat on the long ride home. She woke up in her own bed the next morning and went down to her sister's room, where she found her unresponsive. Her sister had died during the night of meningitis before she could be taken to the doctor. Her parents divorced a year and a half later, which left Patricia reeling with further loss.

During the desensitization of this trauma, Patricia was able to see how her current anxiety stemmed from this childhood experience. She was able to reprocess it with her current emotional skills and abilities. Unknown to her, she had carried some guilt for her sister's death. She understood how that searing memory had not been addressed by her parents, who hid their grief probably out of guilt at not getting her medical help sooner. She was able to have compassion toward herself as well as her parents, whose own divorce probably stemmed from unresolved guilt and grief. *I am safe now* and *I can handle this* became her new positive beliefs when she encountered a garden-variety illness such as a cold or the flu. She was able to process this trauma completely in two sessions. She stayed in therapy for a short time longer just to make sure she was integrating the new insights and positive beliefs about herself and her life.

A Compulsive "High"

Joel was referred to me by another executive because he had crossed boundaries at work and was having an affair with his administrative assistant. It became more complicated as he discovered this woman was already in a relationship with someone else. He admitted that his board of directors and funding sources might ask him to leave the very company he had single-handedly started if they found out. Joel admitted that he'd had many affairs over the years. He explained that it was just part of his personality as a leader who "liked to take risks."

After voluntarily showing me photos of his wife and children, he admitted that his wife was extremely attractive and a great wife and mother. He quickly focused, however, on his affair and his deep attraction to the other woman. Even though he was taking steps to find her another job in another company to avoid a nasty blowup at work, emotionally he was not ready to give up the relationship. He was also not ready to look at the addictive nature of pursuing alluring and forbidden affairs.

Ambivalent about immediately terminating this dangerous liaison, he agreed to not take any more risks in trying to see her during work time, pressuring her in any way, or giving her any more gifts or money. Unfortunately, because he acted so late, he had to "out" himself with his wife regarding the money even though he continued to cover up the actual reason. It took the suspicions of his wife for him to stop this affair, although he never fully admitted it. He also never did the inner work to look at his addictive patterns. Although very relieved that he had gotten off so easily both at work and with his wife, he admitted he wasn't interested in looking more in-depth at the reasons he pursued his "highs" through affairs. He had primarily wanted consultation on how to limit the damage. He did not want to give up his freedom to pursue another affair in the future. He said, "It's part of my risk-taking pleasure!"

Assessing Your Risk-Taking Behavior

When you find yourself wrestling with a compulsive behavior such as Joel's in which you refuse to give up a destructive behavior despite the "close calls," it is time to assess. Compulsive behaviors usually develop over time. Your dopamine-loving brain may seek the "high" your brain gets from anticipation, the unknown and new adventures. High-stress jobs activate the fight-or-flight sympathetic nervous system, which successfully hampers the parasympathetic nervous system's (your prefrontal cortex) ability to assert willpower and long-range planning. There are several warning signs. The following list is made up of the warning signs in Joel's situation:

- keeping his behavior secret
- obsessed with looking forward to the next contact
- feeling that his behavior gave him needed excitement, a "lift"
- dismissing concern from his friends as "exaggerated"
- resisting ending these affairs, as they were an important part of his life
- spending excess money inappropriately, even if in his case he had it
- enjoying the risk associated with having a clandestine relationship
- taking a chance at deeply hurting the people he cared about
- taking a chance at destroying the faith of his business partners
- limiting his intimacy in his primary relationship by lying and cheating

If you assess that many of these are descriptive of your behaviors, then reaching out for help from more than just your friends may be necessary to stop this self-destructive pattern because . . .

You Seek Wholeness Above All Else

Even the Joels of the world desire to live life in an authentic, ethical way despite their internal struggles with giving up a temporary "high." Change can occur when we get tired of the losses—most importantly the loss of our self-worth. There are many losses in situations like this. You can lose relationships, or at the very least, you have to work at length to earn the trust and respect of those you have injured.

If you routinely look at the risk factors and the bottom line in your company decisions, do the same in your personal situations. Many leaders tell me that they wish they had met me a few years earlier because I could have saved them thousands if not millions of dollars in marital settlements by helping them handle the situation at the first signs of trouble.

One executive confided in me that the consequence of his impulsive and addictive patterns resulted in his having to pay two alimony payments of more than $35,000 a month each (not to mention the loss of the $2 to $3 million dollar houses his ex-spouses were granted in their individual settlements).

I hope we all learn from our own mistakes and the mistakes of others. This chapter is devoted to providing a sampling of psychotherapeutic and self-help techniques to show you that change doesn't have to be difficult and that you don't have to go it alone! The majority of professionals extend their help because it is their passion in life. If you feel that your much younger mindset is running your show and sabotaging your leadership success, then read this and the next chapter for pathways to regain your authentic leadership footing.

Healing is not for you alone. You cannot help but directly or indirectly contribute this new outlook, this new state of being to the world. Eckhart Tolle, author of the bestseller *The*

Power of Now, addressed the importance of living from this awakened state:

> All the people you encounter will be impacted. Your state of consciousness gets transmitted to others. One negative person can create a chain reaction of negativity in others. In the same way, a conscious person can dissolve streams of negativity. You affect the underlying collective field of human consciousness. I feel sure that you affect countless others that you never even meet, the collective consciousness of humanity. (Dyer, Wayne, Why Settle for Ordinary? February 4, 2013, http://www. healyourlife.com/author-dr-wayne-w-dyer)

You know of men or women who have used their negative personal experiences to help others, the most famous probably being Oprah Winfrey. How many times have you thought one of your challenging experiences was in a memory box under lock and key only to encounter an opportunity to help another person through a similar situation?

The Healing Path Finds You

If you are open to healing, help is everywhere! This has been an exciting time in history for the development of self-help as well as professional therapeutic techniques. The scientific studies of the brain's reaction to stress and trauma have directed the science of how to heal them. Leaders want results, and many of these approaches are evidence-based therapies. Others anecdotally report success. The following sections are not meant to be a comprehensive list but rather a sampling of tools I routinely use with leaders in their healing. Not every psychotherapist believes that you need to heal all your childhood traumatic memories or negative beliefs to be healthy enough or happy enough in your life. You will intuitively know when you feel stuck in self-defeating patterns or have not been successful in certain areas of your life.

Seeking Professional Help

> *The wound is the place where the light enters you.*
> —Rumi

If your history contains a highly sensitive and emotionally charged episode, or episodes, that gets repeatedly triggered in life's normal routine or if you are experiencing distress in your relationship, health, or career sectors, then professional consultation may help.

For every trauma, there is a way to heal it so that you do not need to carry it with you through life. For every difficult life situation, greater insight into your own self will help improve it. You deserve to regain a greater sense of your trust in life once again. You will come out on the other side a wiser and more skillful leader as well. You deserve to have stable and comforting support to address and transform these traumas into strengths. As you read some of the modalities discussed below, see which ones interest you and might warrant further exploration. There are websites, books, CDs, and online seminars available for each modality.

Significant Healing Modalities

Most psychotherapists or life coaches offer a variety of skills to heal old wounds and strengthen your inner resources. The key for all of us is the awareness of our wounds and their triggers in our lives. Psychotherapists trained in some of the newer techniques believe that engaging the memory system to recall past trauma should always be done with techniques that help one to reprocess and release the negative beliefs. One technique that is now evidence-based in success is EMDR. Another technique that is considered anecdotal based on successful outcomes and is often used by professional life coaches and some psychotherapists is the Emotional Freedom Technique (EFT). Both techniques focus on reprocessing trauma and consequent negative beliefs in a rather short period of time. You may choose to remain in therapy or coaching longer to make sure you are integrating that new belief and awareness in your personal life. I will start with EMDR first.

EMDR Therapy

> *Beliefs about oneself, others and the world could change,*
> *opening up new possibilities for the future.*
> —Francine Shapiro, PhD

EMDR (eye movement desensitization and reprocessing therapy) involves the skills of a trained EMDR therapist. You will need to seek out a psychotherapist trained at a masters or doctoral level at www.emdria.org or inquire about an EMDR certification when you are interviewing prospective therapists.

Dr. Francine Shapiro discovered the phenomena that led her to create the EMDR therapy in 1989. She noted that she felt better after an experience when her eyes darted back and forth when she was thinking of a negative situation. A researcher at heart, she developed a protocol that used eye movements while recalling the trauma and the feelings in the body that worked to desensitize them. The protocol worked successfully to desensitize and reprocess the original emotional feelings and the negative beliefs from the incident. EMDR is now recognized by the American Psychiatric Association, the American Psychological Association, and the U.S. Department of Defense as an effective evidence-based treatment for trauma.

The most profound experiences I have seen of clients' capability of healing negative beliefs and returning to a state of greater wholeness have been when I use EMDR. Leaders who are accustomed to their technology-driven world often prefer working with a light bar where their eyes follow a light back and forth or the handheld tactile "pulsers" that alternately vibrate back and forth in their hands. They also appreciate the speed at which this technique works. Millions of people have been treated by EMDR-trained clinicians around the world. Dr. Shapiro estimates that 84 to 100 percent of traumas can be processed within about three ninety-minute sessions!

As you previously reflected on all the rooms in your house, you learned that negative beliefs often result from earlier negative experiences. These could have been simple disturbing situations or more major traumas, especially with caregivers. EMDR practitioners believe that these intense situations make it difficult for the information processing system to make sense and resolve the situation. The memory is unprocessed. Later, if you have a similar situation happen to you, perhaps with the same or similar type of individual(s), you may feel triggered in this intense way. It is important to remember that if you keep experiencing intense feelings in situations with the same themes, you are exposing an unprocessed past trauma.

Francine Shapiro, PhD, founder of EMDR and author of *Getting Past Your Past: Take Control of Your Life with Self-Help Technique from EMDR Therapy*, writes,

> That's why time doesn't heal all wounds, and you may still feel anger, resentment, pain, sorrow or a number of other emotions about events that took place years ago. They are frozen in time, and the unprocessed memories can become the foundation for emotional, and sometimes physical, problems. Even though you might not have had a major trauma in your life, research has shown that other kinds of life experiences can cause the same types of problems. And since the memory connections happen automatically, below conscious level, you may have no idea what's really running your show. (Shapiro, Francine, "Why Time Doesn't Heal All Wounds", (http://changingminds.org/articles/articles12/time_wounds.htm, Feb. 28, 2012).

One of my clients said she felt her traumatic situation had been isolated in its own sort of jail since she was six. She felt like this six-year-old self was not allowed to have visitors who could shed light on the situation from a mature, healing perspective to get this young memory released once and for all. When she described her isolated unprocessed trauma, she revealed the negative beliefs, a cowering physical posture, and fearful emotions of that developmental stage.

When this isolated trauma is processed with the EMDR technique, the targeted memory is able to make new healing associations with adaptive ideas. For example, these adaptive ideas may relate to how a person survived, other positive experiences he or she forgot, and the regaining one's sense of identity. A person's previous emotional state and understandings of the situation are changed for the better and released. New insights and emotions then replace the old. A common realization is how parents possess their own unhealed traumas, which cause them to be skilled or unskilled in their parenting. If they could have handled the situation differently, they would have.

The trigger that happens in one's current life also lessens or disappears. The "miracle" of this technique is that the client's own brain supplies the needed understandings to bring about the healing release. The EMDR practitioner simply follows the eight-step protocol and intervenes only as necessary to assist with the desensitization and reprocessing.

One client of mine came to therapy because she felt she always had to apologize for any mistake she made at work or in relationships. She felt indebted to anyone who gave her any kind of considerate attention. We processed an incident of her mother slapping her in an alcoholic rage and calling her worthless for breaking a dish. The negative belief she held was *I am bad, worthless.*

Through EMDR, she was able to realize that her mother, who was normally soft-spoken, had been so inebriated that her brain reacted in a violent way to a normal incident. She was able to put her mother's actions into a greater context of her mother having a disease. Even though her mother was often absent, sleeping off her drunken binges, my patient recalled nurturing times with her mother prior to the later stages of alcoholic progression. She accessed an emotional state of gratitude, recalling how lucky she had been that her grandmother had comforted her when possible and finally took custody of her.

Another man felt that his need to work long hours in order to be overly responsible at work was breaking up his marriage. Through EMDR he was able to release his guilt and shame for being at fault for his dad getting drunk and dying in a car accident when he was thirteen. His mother blamed him and his adolescent pranks for the extra stress her husband had been under.

During the EMDR processing, he came to a realization that at age thirteen he could not possibly have been responsible for his dad's death, although his dad had been angry at him for skipping school that day. He realized that his dad's alcoholic lifestyle was something his mother was not able to admit. His feelings of being at fault left him, and his self-compassion was restored. His need to be "overly responsible" at work to prove his worth lessened. He joked around more with his colleagues, and he was able to have a reasonable schedule, which strengthened his marriage.

With EMDR, multiple emotional factors—our innocence, a sense of having put a challenging childhood into perspective, regaining a sense of the good moments in our growing up, a sense of pride perhaps in even surviving it with grace—are also restored in these healing moments. A more peaceful and awakened presence arises from within from true authentic healing and frees you from any confused or low self-worth state.

I heartily recommend that you read Dr. Shapiro's book *Getting Past Your Past*. It is easy to read, full of case examples of people who have been helped and detailed explanations of the EMDR procedure. Helpful suggestions are given with which to approach negative memories and enhance positive self-esteem for use at home. Dr. Shapiro also gives examples of resource-strengthening exercises that can boost your sense of mastery and empowerment. If you are in need of an EMDR-trained therapist, you will receive understanding of the process of healing by reading her examples of problem issues resolved throughout the book.

Emotional Freedom Technique (EFT)

> *You don't have to solve it, only evolve it!*
> —Silvia Hartmann, Energy EFT

EFT (Emotional Freedom Technique) has been called the "people's technique" because it is available to anyone who invests a small amount of time in looking at readily available videos or other online tutorials. You can learn it at home or receive a session from a psychotherapist or coach who uses EFT as a tool. EFT combines Eastern understanding of meridian points and acupressure with Western-based psychotherapy to heal negative beliefs. This procedure has been widely used with families and first responders who witness horrific tragedies such as in Newtown, Connecticut.

There is a simple yet effective protocol to EFT. The protocol consists of tapping with your fingertips on specific meridian points while talking through traumatic or stressful situations and the resulting emotions. Two of the best online sites for resources such as pictures, protocols, and videos are www.emofree.com (Gary Craig's website) and www.thetappingsolution.com by Nicolas Ortner, CEO of The Tapping Solution and creator of a book and documentary by the same name.

Ortner writes in a Huffington Post article "Research suggests that EFT may be so effective because of its perceived ability to balance out the nervous system, leveling off the activity of the parasympathetic and sympathetic regions." The article includes a statement by Dr. Feinstein, a clinical psychologist: "EFT is unusually precise, rapid, and direct for shifting the neurological underpinnings of a range of psychological problems" (Ortner, Nick, Breakthroughs in Energy Psychology: A New Way to Heal the Body and Mind, March 17, 2012).

The Basic EFT Technique

The basic technique places your focus on the negative emotion you are feeling: a recurrent bad memory, unresolved problem, or fear. While focusing on this issue, you use your fingertips to tap six to seven times each of the body's nine meridian points. Tapping on these meridian points while concentrating on resolving the negative emotion prompts your body to process the issue and restore your well-being.

The Nine Meridian Points

Note: Use three to four fingers to tap on point 1 in the following list and one to two fingers to tap on the remaining points 2-9.

1. **Karate chop point:** tap on the edge of your other hand between your wrist and little finger.
2. **Eyebrow:** tap on either eyebrow by the nose where the eyebrow starts.
3. **Outside of eye:** tap on the outside edge of either eye on the bone.
4. **Under eye:** tap just below the center of either eye on the bone.

5. **Under nose:** tap the area below the nose and above the upper lip.
6. **Chin:** tap below the lower lip in the crease where the chin starts.
7. **Collarbone:** tap one or two inches left or right of center on the collarbone.
8. **Under arm:** tap about four inches down from the armpit on the rib cage.
9. **Top of head:** tap around on the top of the head.

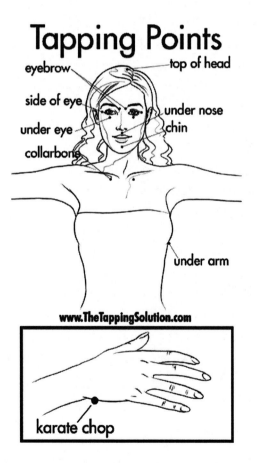

EFT Basic Healing Sequence

Watch the many online tutorials and follow the charts on both www.the tappingsolution.com and www.emofree.com. They are resources that are literally at your fingertips! Below is a short sequence to help you learn the technique:

1. Before you start tapping, identify the problem you wish to heal. For example, "I am afraid of failure in my new business enterprise."

2. Rate the intensity of how you feel about the problem or situation on a scale of zero to ten, with zero being the lowest level of anxiety and ten being the highest. (This enables you to see improvement later on.)

3. Compose a "setup" statement. For example, "Even though I feel tremendous anxiety in taking this risk, I deeply and completely love and accept myself." Or another example could be, "Even though I have tremendous anxiety in making a mistake, I deeply love, accept, and forgive myself."

4. Say the setup statement three times while tapping the karate chop point on the outer side of one hand with the fingers of your other hand. Take a deep breath.

5. With the first two fingers of either hand tap five to seven times on each of the nine meridian points while repeating a simple reminder phrase such as, "My anxiety in taking a risk" or "Don't want to make a mistake" or "I will lose the shirt off my back." Take another deep breath.

6. Focus on your problem again. How intense is the anxiety now compared to the first rating? Give it a rating again from zero to ten. If your anxiety is higher

than a two, you can do another round of tapping, once again starting with your setup statement. You can change your statement to reflect where you are now. For example, "For all the remaining anxiety about taking risks, I deeply and completely accept myself." You have confronted and dealt with the anxiety and negative feelings while giving deep and complete acceptance to yourself. You are now ready to move on to step seven.

7. Install positive feelings by moving into more positive statements such as "I have the strength to take risks" or "There is risk but also a chance for great gains" or "I invested in my dreams."

After completing this sequence, you should notice a considerable drop in anxiety and feel more confident and secure. If not, you may want to dig deeper for the cause of anxiety.

Although I highly recommend watching the many EFT videos on the websites I recommended above for myriad problem areas that could be very similar to yours, I caution you to find the right specific foundational event and the resulting negative belief. Aiming EFT at the right target is important in getting results. It is essential to find your own correct powerful reactions to a past event in order to be released from past and present fears. The many canned EFT scripts on EFT Internet sites are helpful in stimulating your understanding, but they may not address your specific situation.

EFT: Practice Makes Perfect

Online tutorials are highly effective in learning this technique the correct way. Watching them helps you remember the tapping points and language used in addressing your problem area. One of the most important aspects of EFT is the ability to tap away your daily fears and stresses. We take showers and cleanse ourselves every day. Tapping our acupressure points, or meridians, can be a way to cleanse our energy fields so that we have clearer access to our inner peaceful nature.

This technique can be taught to your staff just like any other technique of self-care. You could show the EFT videos at lunchtime as a resource-building technique. As a leader, you may carry high anxiety about making important decisions. This technique may help you release the fear and be clearer about your decision in the privacy of your office or home.

Systemic Therapy: Relationship Therapy

I was trained in family systems therapy in the late '70s, and shortly after that I directed a family therapy clinic at a local university. I have a deep appreciation for the values, rules, and unconscious family systems that affect each of us. Probably one of my favorite systems therapies is the popular relationship approach of IMAGO therapy. Harville Hendrix, PhD, and Helen Hunt, PhD, have written many relationship books, including their very latest, *Making Marriage Simple: Ten Truths for Changing the Relationship You Have into the One You Want* (2013).

On their website, www.gettingtheloveyouwant.com, the authors speak of the unconscious process of seeking a partner who has similar traits to the parent with whom you had the most difficulty:

> You'd think, then, that we would choose someone
> who has what our caretakers lacked. If only that

were so! But the old brain has a mind of its own, with its own checklist of desired qualities. It is carrying around its own image of the perfect partner, a complex synthesis of qualities formed in reaction to the way our caretakers responded to our needs. Every pleasure or pain, every transaction of childhood, has left its mark on us, and these collective impressions form an unconscious picture we're always trying to replicate as we scan our environment for a suitable mate. This image of "the person who can make me whole again" I call the IMAGO.

They continue,

Unfortunately, since we don't understand what's going on, we're shocked when the awful truth of our beloved surfaces and our first impulse is to run screaming in the opposite direction. But that's not all the bad news. Another powerful component of our IMAGO is that we seek the qualities missing in ourselves that got lost in the shuffle of socialization.

The IMAGO approach brings unconscious choices to the consciousness realm level. In a constructive way, you are able to understand what burden you are placing on your partner and how to use the relationship experience to become whole! The questionnaires in the workbooks found on their website allow couples to assume ownership of their part of the issues. Furthermore, you will address the issues of hedonic adaptation spoken about in chapter 2 of this book. IMAGO therapy focuses on the importance of reinventing and reinvesting in your relationship to keep the excitement alive. You don't have to have a troubled relationship to have couple's therapy. In fact, you can absorb more learning and enjoy the process more if there is not a crisis going on!

As a leader, you would not close down part of your business without asking for an analysis by key players. The IMAGO approach ensures that you know all the hidden components of why your relationship may be struggling. Just as in business, it is better to analyze it and intervene sooner rather than later to give it every possible chance of recovering. And if after doing so the relationship is not your ultimate choice, just as in business, you can use the analysis and healing to make a future relationship successful!

Cognitive Behavioral Therapy

> *Between stimulus and response, there is a space.*
> *In that space lays our power to choose our response,*
> *and in our response lays growth and freedom.*
> —Victor Frankl

Cognitive-behavioral therapy (CBT) is a general term for a classification of similar therapies. Rational emotive behavior therapy, dialectic behavior therapy, and mindfulness-based cognitive therapy are three such therapies. These therapies are based on the idea that our thoughts, not external things (specific people or events), cause our feelings, which lead to our behaviors. A CBT therapist can help you identify unhelpful or defeating thinking patterns in your current problems, change inaccurate beliefs, and relate to others in more productive ways.

Mindfulness-based cognitive therapy (MBCT) adds the practice of mindfulness and mindfulness meditation. This is one of the approaches I use in teaching stress management to company leaders. In this practice, you focus on becoming aware of all incoming thoughts and feelings and accepting them but not attaching or reacting to them. You focus instead on acceptance and observation of what is happening without judgment. In chapter 2, you learned how stress can weaken your ability to access your willpower. A practice of MBCT throughout your day can heighten heart variability and greatly lower stress.

Mindfulness means paying attention to your thoughts, emotions, and sensations in each moment and in a nonjudgmental way. It generates self-compassion. Mindfulness helps you shift from a panicked state to a positive one. Your prefrontal cortex has a chance to come back online. The brain loves repeat performances of mindfulness because you generate new neurons to strengthen the practice. It can be helpful to anchor mindfulness with certain behaviors around the office, such as taking a deep breath as you walk through a doorway or down the hallway. Notice what you are feeling, where your thoughts are, and the sensations in your body as you go to a meeting. Breathing deeply into all that awareness and being present can be greatly calming and centering.

A Beginning One-Minute "Noticing" Practice

Find a comfortable seat. Take a breath and close your eyes. Notice the positioning of your body, how you're sitting. Notice if your body is tense or tight and just be aware of it. It is okay if your body is tense or tight. Simply notice that in this moment you are aware of it. Now you are at a choice point. You can make the choice to either soften the muscles, or you can let them be. That is fine. What is your emotional state? Where do you feel your emotions in your body? Can you give them a name? Now go to your thoughts. Is your mind busy or calm in this moment? Distracted or able to focus? Without effort, be aware of your whole body, feelings, and mind. Now open your eyes. What did you notice?

Mindfulness Resources

Jon Kabat-Zinn, founder of the Stress Reduction Clinic at the University of Massachusetts Medical School, has written several books on mindfulness, including *Wherever You Go, There You Are: Mindful Meditations in Everyday Life* and *Mindfulness for Beginners: Reclaiming the Present Moment and your Life*. Eckhart Tolle's book *The Power of Now* complements this practice. His book teaches you to be in the moment with awareness as a way to inner peace and mastery of your stress. While this therapy does not focus on getting to the root of the negative beliefs like EFT and EMDR, the practice of mindfulness helps you strengthen internal control for ever-changing external stressors.

Your Sacred Agenda

If you feel that one or all of these modalities would be helpful for you to heal past events and negative beliefs, read more about them and then reach out to a therapist. Ask the therapist what kind of modalities they use in their approach to your issues.

Psychotherapists who have taken training in EMDR, EFT, IMAGO or other specialties show their willingness to locate the best tools to assist you in strengthening your self-worth and freeing up your potential. When you read the resource books on your own you will feel like part of the therapy "team". There are many self-help and professional healing modalities that I did not list and many more being developed. In an earlier section, I mentioned www.hayhouseradio.com as a resource. By listening to different experts including psychotherapists, life coaches and intuitive coaches, you can learn what philosophy and methods resonate most with you.

Remember that your healing should be at the top of your most sacred agenda. Why would you want to go through life with a heavy sack of negative beliefs thrown over your shoulder? Why would you want to constantly create the same situations for yourself? Even out of the rubble of profound negative experiences you can grow greater self-acceptance, self-love, and a capacity for true intimacy. The ability to manifest goodness in your life and in your company from the power of this authentic alchemical base is immense.

Your healing has a ripple effect to the world around you. If you hold yourself accountable to your highest standards, then you will hold others accountable to their highest standards. If you can change, you will believe that others can heal and change. If you believe in goodness ultimately winning over hatred, then you can help others to do the same. The presence of a saint can be felt the instant that holy person walks into the room. The positive energy of a leader who has truly faced his or her shadow nature and has been healed into wholeness is also intuitively felt in an instant. There is nothing but authenticity to behold.

CHAPTER 6

Leadership Visualization Tools

The world belongs to those who cross many bridges
in their imaginations before others see even a single bridge.
—Chinese proverb

The Company Has a Life of Its Own

Another important tool for leadership is to see your company as a living entity, having an energy force, even a "personality" of its own. I remember the first time I saw the agency I was hired to manage. It was a Sunday, and I was coming for my interview with the board of directors the next morning. The parking lot was empty, and the old red one-story building that housed Goodwill looked tired, worn out, and run-down. I parked on the far side of the parking lot and slowly walked across the cracked and broken asphalt. Weeds grew in many of the cracks. The cracks looked like wrinkles, and the potholes and broken surface resembled acne. Stopping at the front door, I read a sign: *Goodwill Industries, since 1925.* She looked every bit her age.

In my first days at the agency, I felt her energy. I could feel her fatigue, but I never thought of actually "listening" and even "speaking" to her about what she needed to heal. I wrote strategies and plans. I met with all the employees, listened, and plotted ways to help infuse new life and energy into the agency. In nautical terms, she was badly listing. Financially she was deeply in debt, and operationally she was not in a sustainable position. In my first week on the job, our financial officer told me it would be difficult to meet payroll and asked my opinion.

"We don't have the money to meet payroll?" I asked, somewhat amazed. He shook his head and told me it was often a timing issue as we waited for payment from the state for providing contract work to individuals with disabilities. "Do we have a reserve?" I asked. Again he shook his head. I asked him to sit and tell me all he could about the fiscal situation of the agency, which he did.

Beyond the fiscal crisis the agency was in, it suffered from even a deeper problem: it had no spirit, no energy . . . and my employees and stakeholders felt it as well.

When I was much younger, I had a practice of writing letters and then answering them. My dad was not a very "present" father, often having to work long hours to raise my brothers and me, and I often wrote to him, telling him how I was feeling or what I was wondering about the many issues of life young boys have. I never gave him the letters, as I wasn't sure if he would just laugh or if he would even read them, but it helped to write them nonetheless. I often poured my heart out in them. As I grew older, I started writing letters to girls I liked or even to my older brothers, who were busy and not always involved in my daily life. I even wrote letters to God, asking questions that bothered me.

The letter writing helped me. It got issues off my chest and onto paper if nothing else. Gradually, however, something began to happen with my letters. I would write them, and within a day or a few days I would start "hearing" answers concerning the issues I wrote about. As a teenager, I once wrote a letter to Anne, a young girl down the street who I liked very much. In the letter, I wrote that I liked her and thought she was pretty. A couple of days later, I heard a voice in the hallway at school. I turned around to see who it was, and it was Anne!

We began a friendship that lasted several years in school, and my memory of her all these years later is still pleasant and warm. Had she somehow heard or understood the words I had written to her?

I experimented with others in the same way . . . teachers, people I wished to befriend, coaches I wished would let me play sports. I even wrote tough questions to God about the nature of events happening around me. I not only became more and more amazed about the results these letters provided, but in time I even started answering them as if I were those people.

Years later, I began to write to Goodwill. I would get to the office before anyone came to work, and I would sit at the computer and write her letters. After a few frustrating, even fearful, weeks at Goodwill, I still remember the content of the first letter I wrote.

> *I feel your sadness and emptiness*, I wrote. *I sense that you are sick and need help. So help me. Talk to me. I will listen if you do. Tell me what you need.*

It was like a prayer. I finished the letter and sent it to myself as an e-mail. I felt "sending" the letter was important. I sat for a moment and was readying myself to start checking bank accounts and get ready for the tasks of the day when an overwhelming sadness came upon me. It felt as though a tremendous burden was pressing me down into my chair.

> I became alarmed. Maybe I was having a heart attack or a stroke! I took a drink of water and almost dropped the cup. Even the cup felt heavy. I started to sweat, and my hands trembled. I felt my throat tighten and tears well in my eyes. Every effort I made to get hold of myself seemed to fail. I was falling apart, sitting alone at my desk in the early morning.

That's how Goodwill spoke to me. I had asked, and she answered. It took me several days to sort out all the emotions of that morning, but gradually I did. In the weeks that followed, I learned that this agency had its own sense of awareness. I learned that she had *much* to tell me, and I began to listen. Not only did I listen, but I asked questions, always in the form of written letters.

I learned from that first connection that the agency not only felt sad and weary, but she felt betrayed by past leadership. She felt ignored by management and staff.

As much as I needed to deal with the daily issues, the agency wanted to keep telling me how she felt. I would even fight back at times and tell her I didn't have time for this, but she persisted. She wanted me to feel her emotions, and I gradually came to learn that she wanted me to connect with and feel how she felt.

When the "feelings" descended on me at the office, I would simply leave. I began taking walks that first summer, and as I walked, we talked. She needed to communicate with me, the leader, and I felt she took *every* opportunity to do so!

Collective Consciousness

Companies have consciousness, lives of their own. They have histories and missions, purposes and responsibilities. Not like people, obviously, but they are a collection of every employee, every client or consumer, every customer, and every board member or member of management from their very beginning to the present. I no longer get caught up in definitions, for I have learned there is far too much for me to comprehend and understand or try to define . . . Yet I can still feel.

When I focus on the collective consciousness of a nation such as Uganda, where 50 percent of the adults in the country are HIV positive and 25 percent are living with full-blown AIDS, I feel "her" pain. When I focus on the collective anger of political or religious entities, such as the radical Islam, I feel their anger and outrage. All of us can feel these rivers of anger, sadness, intolerance, greed, or joy.

Good leaders listen. They listen to their management teams, their customers, their community leaders, their employees, and their clients; however, really "in-touch" leaders learn to listen to their companies' voices as well.

What Does Your Company Need?

Once you connect with your company's needs and its voice, your purpose becomes clearer. You are there as the leader to serve her, first and foremost. Your management team might have a voice. They will work on you to "buy" their ideas, their strategies, and their planning, but a wise and authentic leader seeks first only one voice. What does your agency need? What path does she wish to take? Most of all, she needs a champion: you.

Today in my leadership position, all major decisions are filtered through that voice. I cannot define what this Goodwill's consciousness is, how it communicates, or how it wishes to serve our communities and the people in them, but she desires to be served. In return, she serves. It is the reason for her existence. Offering opportunities to individuals with disabilities or shoppers in need or donors who wish to give is her purpose. It is her heartbeat . . . and I have learned to listen.

Visualization

A powerful leadership tool is the ability to "see" the end result. Visualization is creating a mental picture of an outcome you would like to achieve. It is a powerful tool because it allows the brain to believe that the outcome has already been achieved.

Napoleon Hill stated, "You have to see yourself in abundance, feel it, and dwell in it." (*Think & Grow Rich*, March 30, 2013). Esther Hicks expressed it a bit differently when she said we cannot help but create new visions because out of contrast or desire we automatically "send rockets of desire into the Universe!" (*Getting Into The Vortex: Guided Meditations CD and User Guide*, Nov 15, 2010) Our only job is to "allow" these creations to come into existence through the magnetic draw of a positive state of being. A belief in our worth, holding a view of life as an Earth school of valuable lessons, and gratitude for the present give great magnetizing or "pulling" power to our creations or dreams.

The law of attraction affirms, "That which is like unto itself is drawn," (*The Law of Attraction*, Esther and Jerry Hicks, Dec. 1, 2006). which means vibrations are always matched. So as you experience the contrast that inspires the new idea within you, this new idea—this desire—whether it is a strong one or a soft one, is summoning unto itself proportionately. And as it summons, it is always answered. It is the basis of our universe: when it is asked, it is always given. The confusion humans feel is that they think they are asking with their words—or even with their actions—and sometimes they are. But the universe is not responding to your words or your actions. The universe is responding to your "vibrational calling," according to Abraham as channeled by Esther Hicks (http://www.abraham-hicks.com). *Contrast* is feeling the difference between what you currently experience and what you would rather experience. When you have a headache, you long for relief from pain. When you cannot pay your bills, you long for plenty of money in your bank account. It is the desire for something different in your life that inspires the new idea. Your life should be filled with abundance. You should belong in a loving relationship and family. Life should present itself this way to us all. So why doesn't it? There is something wrong, and what is wrong is within you, not outside you, no matter what it looks like.

Visualizing a Payroll that I Didn't Have

I recall vividly the week that began with an overdrawn bank account at my agency. Starting a payroll week overdrawn was not a good practice, and I immediately knew we'd have a problem. While talking with my finance staff, I quickly realized that expensive insurance premiums had been paid, and those checks had overdrawn the account. Then I learned that another large payment of more than $20,000 hadn't even cleared yet.

I called my banker. I dread these types of calls. It brings out deep insecurity: *I'm not a good CEO* or *I can't manage my own agency's money.* No matter the insecurity, I've learned that honesty is the best policy. Being forthright with your board, your employees, your spouse, or in this case, your banker is always best.

"So, I'm thinking I won't be able to meet payroll this week," I began after a few necessary salutations. "Oh and why not?" he asked in banker style. I gave him plausible explanations and told him it simply was a timing problem. I needed him to cover my payroll that week.

"How much are we talking about?" he asked. "Well, about $35,000. Maybe more," I replied sheepishly.

"$35,000?" he repeated slowly. "You know, Steve, I can't do this," he finally said. My heart sank. My world was collapsing. If I couldn't pay my employees, it meant the end of days, the final curtain call, perhaps, even front-page news!

"Kevin," I begged, "it is a timing issue. I'll have it covered by early the next week." He listened and finally said, "Well, it's only Tuesday. Transfer everything you can. We've got until Friday. Make it happen, Steve. I'll see what I can do to cover you, but I can't promise we won't send checks back."

That was a long week for me, a very long week. Thursday morning came, and we were short by $36,270. I had been off by only $1,200. We couldn't meet our next day payroll.

All week I sat with Sharon, my wife. We had been visualizing that a solution would come and that my agency wouldn't fold in disgrace or shame for not being able to pay my employees. "Believe in the purpose of this agency," she offered. "Think of how it serves your staff, of the disabled people it serves. Believe that if it is for good, all higher powers love to find a way to help in these situations." I listened intently. "Spirit will find a way," she continued. "You only need to believe and see it finished, see it whole, see it done."

Spirit will find a way? All higher powers love to help good causes? Did I believe that much? Did I really believe that much in the unseen world that help could come in the most material way? My payroll could really be covered? There was no doubt that Sharon's belief far exceeded my own. I was more of a Sunday morning believer. Could I really hand this over to a benevolent higher consciousness and hope for a solution?

That night I lay in bed and stayed as positive as I could. I thought about how this agency had served people for eighty-four years and thought of all the disabled people, the customers, the staff it was presently serving. I visualized us somehow getting past this situation, and with warm thoughts toward Mother Goodwill, I simply surrendered. I hadn't seen how this could end in anything but an ugly, shaming, and embarrassing front-page story, yet I gave it all to God and went to sleep.

At work the next morning, I opened the bank account. We had overdrawn by $36,270. I left a voice mail message to my banker, who hadn't arrived at work yet, admitting I hadn't found a solution.

Two hours later, my finance clerk came in with a smile on her face. She handed me a check for services we'd rendered to a large account. I opened it as she stood before me, the check amount . . . $36,382! Spirit had found a way to toss an extra $112 into my account!

Gratefully, I took the check and deposited it. Kevin and the bank were happy, but I wasn't just happy; I was dumbfounded in my joy. How could I not have believed? How could I have doubted that Spirit would show the way and give me a $112 tip?

Visualization is a powerful leadership tool. So powerful, in fact, that it can change outcomes. It can change our future. Add to it the power of belief, and there is little one cannot achieve. Whether an employee payroll or a cataclysmic event—visualize your future, your desire, your need, and your wants . . . Spirit will provide.

Beliefs that Attract Good Stuff
By Sharon

Steve asked, "How could I not believe?" For starters, as in this example, it is difficult to believe when everything looks insurmountable! Visualization is a wonderful tool, yet you may feel unsure about even the appropriateness of visualization when you are faced with daunting circumstances. Shouldn't you focus on the problem instead? When you are in doubt, where do you begin?

Incremental steps are always best . . . starting small. In order to visualize, I begin by stating personal beliefs that allow me to increasingly view the situation in a more positive light. About four years ago, I began making a personal list of these "universal" beliefs. I gathered them over time by writing them on little slips of paper as I read an inspirational book or even heard lyrics in a song. They made sense to me and gave me hope.

Here I offer the beliefs that resonated with me and helped me feel that I could authentically visualize a positive outcome without lying to myself. These beliefs are part of a book on beliefs that I am in the process of writing. Try them on for size. Is this your belief? Do you have a different or better one for yourself? Does it help you with a situation you are troubled by? Take my practice of writing your beliefs down and build your own "belief book." (Feel free to share them with me with the contact information I have provided at the back of the book.

Sharon's Nine Beliefs

Belief 1
I am born of the love in the Universe. I am a spiritual being in a human form; therefore, I am loved and provided for beyond anything I could ever imagine.

Belief 2
There is nothing I could *ever* do to be outside the unconditional love in which I am forever held. My Creator views any negative behavior on my part as having arisen from fear and my forgotten connection with my Creator.

Belief 3
Events are useful mirrors for me to see the reflection of what needs healing within myself. A negative money situation may reflect a subconscious belief in my feelings of lack. An unfulfilling relationship may be a reflection of my low self-esteem.

Believe 4
Reciprocity—I can expect goodness to enter my life on the level of my mastery. For example, if I have mastered self-love, I can expect at least that level of love from another because I will be able to accept it. If I have respect and mastery of money along with a generous spirit, I can expect that the energy of money will want to flow to me.

Belief 5
I have the best truth for myself within my own heart. I am meant to follow my own individual truth at each moment in

time. My truth and other's inner truth are constantly evolving as I understand myself, others, and situations from different experiences. Everyone's truth is to be respected. Their truth serves them as they evolve in their consciousness.

Belief 6
I have a life purpose that only I can fulfill in my unique, creative way. I am meant to use my talents for the joy of my expression and the good of others. Because this is my higher self's work, blessed by my Creator, I will be given opportunities and support for the self-expression that delights and inspires me.

Belief 7
The nature of love is to bless me with bounty. Faith allows these blessings to come to me. Any positive service to others is totally funded in all ways by grace.

Belief 8
I am one with all others. My feelings and actions affect all others and all life on this planet. Every cell in my body and every atom on Earth contains the oneness that we all are. Increasing my self-worth uplifts others.

Belief 9
I have the gift of free will. I will always know if I am using it for good by how loving my thoughts and actions are. I have the power to raise others up through my thoughts and actions.

———·———

From Belief, We Change Our Outcome

Often our first sign of using our beliefs like the ones that Sharon provided above is when we begin to see changes in people's responses and the events around us. What has happened to the outside world, we ask. Is it changing, or are we changing? The answer will be both, of course. Persistent positive vibrational thoughts and a deep belief in your worthiness will bring results to your life. Job promotions find their way to us, and addictive behaviors fall by the wayside. Old patterns of self-deprivation and self-anger and shame are packed away, never to return. You start to make better choices in your daily life, all because you have moved from a negative belief or view of life to a more positive one.

From Feeling Invisible . . .

I grew up in a family with three older brothers. They were all talented in many different ways. I often felt invisible, as though I didn't matter as much. By the time I entered middle school, I had withdrawn so much that I felt insignificant, as if I had no identity of my own.

I recall one occasion when I was challenged to ask a girl to dance at a middle school dance night. Mustering all the courage I could, I painstakingly walked across the dance floor and stood motionless before her and her friends, not even knowing what to say to her. When she looked up and saw me, she asked, "Where did you come from?" She hadn't even noticed me before. I managed to blurt out that I'd like to dance with her, at which she laughed and told me to go back and sit down. I was crushed! Even worse, I had to make the long walk back across the gymnasium floor to the hoots and catcalls of my "friends," who sat laughing at my humiliation.

Three years later, when I was still feeling invisible and not worthy of attention, my dad changed jobs and had to move sixty miles away to a smaller town. I was entering my senior year of high school, and the last thing I wanted to do was change schools and move! I remember then confessing to my older brother John how I'd felt during all those young teenage years. He was surprised and saddened to hear me describe myself as invisible, plain, not special in any way, and he gave me some important advice: "This fall, go with a new attitude. No one knows you. You can be and do anything you want because no one will know the difference."

. . . To Being Visible

I thought about it, and although fearful, I walked into my new high school on a September day with new hope, a big smile, and a healing belief that I didn't want to be invisible any longer. Within days, the world began to change and open up for me. I was asked out on a date during my first week! When several young women called me handsome, I was shocked! I tried out for the class play, hoping for a small part, and was cast in the leading male role. I tried out for the baseball team, showing new confidence, and became the starting pitcher for the senior high team; I went on to win several games, earning a coveted sports letter in baseball. It was a simple confirmation that I was special and that I wasn't invisible.

The world had not changed for me; I had changed for it by healing a long-held negative belief. As I grew more confident within my own skin, more opportunity came to me. I still remember one of the headlines in the local paper that read: "Transfer student might be Raiders' [baseball team] hope." I played three sports, excelled in drama and debate, got straight A's, and was as popular as I cared to be. It was an amazing year that taught me something very important: As we change, the world changes around us. As we heal, the world becomes a more joyful and potential-filled place in which to live.

I met my leader on the road, walking toward me with open arms, welcoming me. I learned that if I could heal that negative belief, I could heal others, and as I did, the world opened up more and more until I felt like a kid in a huge playground of opportunity.

As you meet yourself on the road, all of your senses grow sharper. You walk more confidently and show more concern for others and less for yourself. As the onion layers are peeled away, you are less self-absorbed, less tense, and less worried.

Then an amazing thing happens. One day, you become the leader—positive, bountiful, strong, confident, and good. More opportunity comes your way, and others around you begin calling you "lucky" or "golden." But you know better. The changes around you happen as though you are in a whirling hologram of potential. As you wave your arms and ask for a different reality to present itself to you, guess what? It does!

Pure Intended Thought—Using the "Mind Field"

A relatively new theory called *quantum mind* and described by physician and writer Deepak Chopra in his book *Life after Death, The Burden of Proof (November 17, 2006)* states that the human brain is not the center of creative thought at all; it merely acts like a receiver, much like your radio is not the source of music. Chopra describes a conscious "mind field" from which we all can access information and creative thought and obtain any outcome to any problem we "select" from the quantum mind field. What if every outcome to any human situation is already available to us simply by "tuning" our receivers, our human brains, into receptivity of the outcome desired in the mind field?

The chair you are sitting on began as a thought in someone's mind. So did the house or apartment you occupy, the dishes you eat from, and the radio or television you listen to. Someone imagined the design, placed every detail of it on drafting paper or planned it as a computer model, and then built it. Everything begins in thought. There are few accidents when it comes to creation. The intent to create is simple enough.

Intending Our Thoughts: Firing Our Neurons

Thought is the preamble to creation, and it is the key ingredient to the creation of anything. By themselves, thoughts are not manifested creation; they only serve as the precursor to creation. With intention, however, thought begins to form, molding itself toward living material substance. At some point, the idea graduates into a form that can be drawn, molded, shaped, or erected.

A human being has about 100 billion brain cells. Although different neurons fire at different speeds, as a rough estimate it is reasonable to estimate that a neuron can fire about once every five milliseconds, or about two hundred times a second. Brain waves have been measured traveling an average of 120 meters per second. The messages your brain creates—to tell your body to move—travel at more than 1,700 mph. Needless to say, our thoughts occur fast and often.

Thoughts can be powerful energy, and it is good to know that most of our thoughts will never manifest into concrete form. If thoughts of anger, lust, or frustration were to suddenly be seen and heard by others, we would all be in real trouble during our daily lives! Intended thought, however, can manifest into form and often does. Intention is the energy that sets thought into motion, and the strength and duration of the intention ultimately determines the ability for thought to manifest itself.

The Minnesota Experiment

On a recent trip I took with my brother Phil, we were driving 1,500 miles home after two weeks of fishing in northern Minnesota. We were tired, hadn't shaved, and probably didn't look too sharp. We had been talking about this book and "pure intended thought" and decided to test the concept. We spent a few minutes raising our emotional energy and went into a Bob Evans to see if we could affect the moods and behaviors of others around us—others we had never met.

From the moment we entered, we addressed the hostess and wait staff with warmth and honesty. We kept all of our comments and thoughts pure and as high energy as we could without sounding trite or insincere. Immediately we were met with the same energy—smiles and comments of how nice we were. These attitudes and comments came not only from the wait staff, but other patrons took notice as well. Before long, the restaurant's manager came out to meet us. We were honestly complimentary of his wait staff, which made them all feel even better. We commented on the freshness of the food and the delicious taste. All of our comments were authentic and true.

We looked at everyone in that restaurant as though they were angels and treated them with respect, courtesy, fun, and friendliness. When we asked about the cooks, they came to meet us. We thanked them. Customers saw the genuineness of our comments and shared their smiles and also their compliments. We noticed the energy of separateness that existed when we entered the restaurant had dissipated, and now diners in separate booths were sharing laughs and enjoying the moment as more and more of us began speaking together.

As we left the restaurant, some of these new friends said good-bye. The wait staff and management also thanked us for a wonderful experience. Smiles and warm good-byes escorted us as we left. The experiment seemed to work well.

For the Highest Good

We attract to us the emotional thoughts we hold within us. A happy person draws positive friends to him or her rather than somber ones. Playful people draw other fun-loving friends to them, and successful people also draw other successful individuals to themselves in the same fashion.

An everyday example of pure intended thought is the power of prayer in a congregation that prays for the welfare of another. Pure intended thought has no measure of personal gain attached to it. We "intend" for the good of our clients, our customers, and our employees. Our goal is their highest good, and our emotionally charged intention grows in energy and manifestation when we keep personal gain out of leadership. This is servant leadership.

We see examples of this in sports all the time. Before a big game, athletes huddle around each other and transmit energy between them by shouting, praying, clapping, slapping hands, and even dancing. Soon the collective intention is shared by all—the shared intended thought to perform well.

Why don't we do this more in business? Why don't we huddle on Monday mornings and lead those who are somber and depressed into a higher energy? Why are staff meetings uninspiring, dull, and boring when they could be charged with energy, slapping hands, shouting, or even dancing like athletes do before the start of a big game? Does it help? Of course it does! Anyone who has been a part of a collective team effort focused on the energy and high of winning through collective huddles knows how effective this energy is! We get pumped, enthusiastic, charged, and motivated.

Pure intention is a powerful tool in leadership. When energy is applied to the purest intentions, thought begins to gel, gains momentum, and moves closer to creative reality. When intention is shared by like minds, the effects become magnified.

CHAPTER 7

The Alchemy of Pure Intuition

> *The intuitive mind is a sacred gift and the rational mind*
> *is a faithful servant. We have created a society that honors*
> *the servant and has forgotten the gift.*
> —Albert Einstein

E ffective leaders trust their hunches and listen for synchronistic answers to their problems in the world around them. Call it "gut" or "inner knowing," intuition is a powerful tool and ally for leadership. It serves you well in all areas of your life.

I remember an incident in my family years ago that illustrates this. As a boy, I had a hidden fort in the rafters of our attic. To reach it, I had to scramble along the rafters on my knees until I reached a section of plywood that covered the rafters and served as the floor of my hideout. One day, my mother was at a neighbor woman's house and had no idea, of course, where I was.

As I squatted along the attic rafters, I suddenly slipped and fell into the insulation and right through the floor of the attic and the ceiling of the upstairs bedroom below me. As I fell, I hit my head on one of the rafters and came crashing down into a heap on the bedroom floor, temporarily knocked unconscious.

Little did I know, at that moment my mother felt a rush of panic and told the neighbor woman something was wrong. She dashed out of the house and ran home. Without even hearing a sound from me, she ran up the steps to the upstairs bedroom and found me lying on the floor, pride a bit wounded but otherwise okay. To this day I wonder how she knew! From three houses away, she felt my panic and knew what to do as she rushed home to find me. The power of intuition is truly remarkable. It is not possessed solely by mothers but is a natural gift we all possess. We must develop it and learn to trust in it, through good times and difficult ones.

Your Own Inner Voice

This section on intuition is written by Sharon

As a psychotherapist, business coach, and someone who possesses proven intuitive abilities, I love to teach intuitive skill building in a variety of settings, from medical to business. Business intuition is about matching your inner wisdom with your logical mind and problem-solving skills. They are powerful partners.

Intuition supports you to keep on a chosen path because you know it is right to hold to that course for now. That same inner knowing can tell you to change course, continue to do more of what works, or release what doesn't. Acting on your intuition can save time and money and prevent failure. Intuitive information processing strategies are found today in many of Fortune 100 and 500 companies.

Taking an Intuitive Shortcut

> *Your time is limited; don't waste it living someone else's life.*
> *Don't be trapped by dogma, which is living the result of other people's*
> *thinking. Don't let the noise of others' opinion drown your own inner*
> *voice. Everything else is secondary.*
> —Steve Jobs

Webster says intuition is "instantaneous apperception" and "the power of attaining direct knowledge without evident rational thought." It comes from the Latin word *intuera*, which means "to look within." Our evolutionary "wiring for survival" still serves us. Our intuitive body reacts to danger first in a gut reaction, second in a heart reaction, and third and lastly in the brain. In that moment of danger, we receive input from both the left and right brain, input from all five senses, and then input from our own unique life experience to put our understanding in place.

Shortcuts in any business process are embraced if they lead to saving time and the almighty bottom line. Intuition is that shortcut, and more importantly, it can be a second validation of your own logical process. This is why we are devoting an entire chapter to it.

Reasons for Becoming an Intuitive Leader

When you develop a method to listen to your intuition, you have a greater ability to:

- *Validate that "inner knowing" that your business is on track and you are making the right decisions. A strong sense of* business intuition can even outweigh external evidence that might lead you to a different decision. Your inner sense can help you stay the course to eventual success—the sense that you are right where you are supposed to be and doing exactly what you should be doing.

- *Set strategic direction that is in alignment with a greater truth.* Often leaders make decisions because they "believe" it is in the greater good, not just for the immediate best interest of the business. When leaders make inner decisions based on solid values, they can trust that their higher selves' intuitive voices and the synchronistic occurrences around them will join to support that vision.

- *Value and listen to the intuitive ideas and thoughts of others as well.* Families do this all the time. Effective leaders learn to trust employees who act from their intuitive abilities, and they value the creative ideas that come from them.

- *Utilize intuition in hiring the right type of person or securing the best business relationships for your business.* Who is the right employee for the job? Who is not? Who can be trusted? Effective leaders look deeper than resumes and experience. They rely on their inner knowing and their inner truth for these often difficult and crucial human decisions in business.

- *Monitor progress.* Intuition is like your internal weather vane, and when it shifts with the variations of internal energy, your direction may need to shift with it.

- *Invent great things.* Creative ideas always come through intuitive channels.

Develop a Method to Listen to Your Intuition

Intuition becomes increasingly valuable
in the new information society precisely
because there is so much data.
—John Naisbitt

All successful leaders, perhaps even unwittingly, have developed their own methods to access their intuition. Thomas Edison is reported to have sat in a chair, holding a ball in each hand while thinking of a problem for which he needed a solution. He would then proceed to daydream. When he was about to fall asleep, the balls would drop to the floor, causing him to abruptly become alert. He would immediately write down any ideas or dreams he was having. He accessed his inventive ideas and solutions in these moments. Edison knew that intuition is found in the fearless present moment with no past or future to corrupt it; therefore, creativity has no limits. Leaders such as Edison would then and only then use their logical minds and experiences to evaluate whether the new idea was one they could put into action. Intuition and the logical mind truly make a great team.

The beauty of your intuition is that it is like a good partner: It won't send mixed messages or ask you to go against your inner truth! You are permitted to review your intuitive hunch over and over without getting impatient! It doesn't engage you in wishful thinking or unrealistic dreams. It just feels right!

Your Intuitive Voice Speaks Its Own Language

Your intuitive voice works to warn you of a negative situation in the following ways:

- Your emotions flatten when you hear a bad idea. The idea goes *thunk* instead of *ping!*
- You repeatedly have a thought cross your mind.
- Everything *should* be okay with the plan, but something in one of your five senses says no. Somehow it doesn't smell, feel, hear, or look okay.
- You feel yourself avoiding moving forward on something, literally dragging your feet.
- You get a gut reaction, perhaps an awful feeling in the pit of your stomach, goose bumps, a shiver, or a chilled feeling up your spine whenever you think about it.
- You feel anxious or motivated to move on something quickly and you are not sure why.
- You feel very stressed, burned out, achy, or emotionally upset, or you have tense headaches, all of which signal that change is needed!

On the other hand, your intuitive voice works to endorse a positive move in the following ways:

- You get an "aha" or an instant hit of a solution to a problem when you are doing something mindless, such as going for a walk or taking a shower.
- You notice synchronistic events happening around you to support your new idea.
- You know who is calling before you answer the phone.

- You get the idea to call or walk over and talk to someone.
- You get a warm, positive feeling inside when you think of an idea.
- You feel that you need to act on an idea even though you're not sure why.
- The intuitive thought that crosses your mind appears as if it came from outside of your normal thinking, perhaps seeming "other worldly" or "out of the blue."

Believe in Your Inner Guidance and the Synchronicities that Happen!
By Sharon

I am called the "Believe Coach" because I assist others in believing in their worth and assist in the alignment of all that exists to support their journeys. I help my clients stay calm in the current moment and respond to cues that feel aligned with their higher purposes. Believing in your purpose helps you stay the course when the process feels challenging.

Through my six years of being single after my divorce, my motto was "Be your own best friend!" If you want a great relationship, make sure you are capable of having one with yourself first! My motto was broken into three parts: self-truth, self-kindness, and self-expression in my own life. Despite some of my friends' misgivings at my staunch belief in the outcome of finding a mate, I knew that if I did my inner work, it would be easier to hold my positive visualization of him. I knew I would be able to accept an equal relationship and value it!

Sometimes when we are taking shortcuts in life, we feel we don't "deserve" our dreams. We know we are waiting for someone or something to rescue us, to compensate for our lack of happiness. During those years, I focused on building a life that was full of joy and self-expression. I didn't want to depend on waiting for the right mate in order to be happy in life. I knew I didn't want a mate who was doing that either. It is too much responsibility! I also had to trust in the right timing. Every time I would ask, "Is this the right time to meet him?" I would intuitively hear, "You're not done yet," and I would keep on going with all that I was doing.

Deciding this time against using online dating, I simply surrendered the perfect timing and way of meeting him. All I asked was that our first meeting be fun and humorous!

In February 2010, I boarded a Southwest flight for Kansas from Nashville never having flown that airline before. I realized that my C group queue number, obtained at the last minute upon arriving at the airport, was the last to board. My gate attendant took my boarding pass, and I realized I was meant to have memorized the seat/queue number on it. Thinking this was a system that could be a bit risky for passengers such as myself who forget where their cars are parked in the parking lot, I chanted this number all the way back to my seat, C16!

I was feeling very proud that I had remembered my number only to discover a tall, long-legged man already sitting in my seat with his feet splayed out in the aisle! I firmly but politely told this relaxed, sleepy looking man that he was in the wrong seat, but he didn't budge. When I started becoming more vocal, he quickly realized that I was clueless about the first-come, first-served no-seat assignment policy on this airline. To the deer-in-the-headlights woman before him, he suggested the only remaining seat beside him and without further ado took my little red suitcase and hoisted it into the carry-on compartment above.

Without further argument, I conceded because the airline attendant motioned that the plane needed to leave. After all, he did have very long legs and probably needed that aisle seat. Seated but still feeling a bit put upon, I pulled out my book, *The Alchemist*, and began to read. He remarked, "Good book!" and pulled out his own book by the same author. A two-hour conversation ensued. That awkward start was the beginning of a romantic soul-mate connection that continued onward to marriage. This book is one of our cocreations.

Don't Just Listen: Act on Your Intuition!
Written by Steve

As a young newspaperman in my early career, I worked for an old time-worn yet superb editor named Bill Macklin. I was young and full of ideas for stories to write in the small conservative town the weekly newspaper served. Each idea I presented to Bill would wrinkle his face in deep furrows, either drawing a scowl or a wry smile. The story ideas he didn't like brought both expressions. Finally, in desperation and as a last resort I asked for help.

"Well now, there's a place to start," he growled. "Maybe you might have thought of asking for advice a while back."

Embarrassed but undaunted, I pressed on. "You don't like me much, do you?" I asked, to which he replied, "Son, you wouldn't be here talking to me if I didn't like you. You have promise, but you don't know the first thing about writing." I took offense to his comment but tried hard not to show it. I had a college degree and had worked hard to hone my craft, none of which mattered to Bill.

"You have to write from your gut," he then told me. "You have to quit thinking and begin to 'feel' what people need and want to read." I looked at Bill like a deer in the headlights. "Feel?" I inquired. "Feel what people need to read?" He nodded and gave me that old wry smile. "Yep, feel it in your gut."

I struggled long enough to learn the craft, that is for sure, but I never forgot his advice. Harnessing the power of our inner truth, that inner knowing . . . that "gut" feeling is something I have come to believe in strongly over the years.

Many years later, I was absorbed in the problems of my agency as president, and I decided I needed a walk. I walked and walked as I sorted out the issues, and there were many in the agency where I had just started working. I walked until I realized that I'd grown hungry, so I stopped at a supermarket to see if I could get a sandwich. At the pizza counter, I ordered, and then I noticed a man sitting alone at one of the tables. He wore dirty sweatpants and a dirtier sweatshirt. His face was covered with stubble, and his graying hair looked as though it hadn't been washed in quite a while.

I paid for my piece of pizza and took a table on the far side of the lunchroom area. Even from there I could detect a faint smell of gasoline coming from the man. Had he just come from a nearby dumpster, I asked myself. But as I ate, preoccupied in my thoughts, I couldn't help but hear a loud voice in my head: *Go and talk to that man. He is important.* Initially I dismissed it, but I have come to learn that when I hear a persistent inner voice calling to get my attention, I should listen.

I picked up my pizza, got up, walked over to the man, and asked if I could join him. "Sure, have a seat," he said, a bit alarmed that a man in a suit would want to join him when there were six empty tables nearby. "I'm not sure why I need to meet you," I began, "but I think it's important I introduce myself to you."

For the next thirty minutes I sat spellbound as Ronnie told me that he specialized in recycling waste and trash. He knew the price of waste plastic, glass, cardboard, and metals. When I told him I was president of the local Goodwill and had tons of this material I was paying top dollar to dispose of in the local landfill, his face crinkled up like old Bill Macklin's, and he sort of scowled. "You need a guy like me to help you. Everything has value," he said. "Everything . . . and I can save you a lot of money."

Ronnie has become my equivalent of an environmental engineer and has worked for me since. He started recycling programs and has found outlets for trash and waste I never knew existed. When I offered him a salary, he wrinkled up his face, smiled in Macklin style, and said, "I'll just take a cut of all this lovely waste you've been burying."

Ronnie still dresses in dirty old sweatpants and sweaters three layers thick. One of my staff gave him the affectionate name of Oil Can Ronnie. He always looks like he wades through thousands of pounds of my recycling material to check it all out personally, but he doesn't care, and neither do I. Ronnie is saving me thousands of dollars and making money for me and for him by his simple expression, "Everything has value."

The power of "gut" and intuition for leaders can't be stressed enough as a tool of leadership. Learn to trust your intuitive voice within, for you never know what person, place, or thing you will meet next that can open doors and change your life or business.

Guidelines for Enlivening Your Intuition
Written by Sharon

> *People who lean on logic and philosophy and rational exposition*
> *err by starving the best part of the mind.*
> —William Butler Yeats

The following exercises will assist you in unlocking and enlivening your valuable intuitive voice as well as the voices of your employees. High-achieving leaders tend to over judge and second-guess their intuitive hits. These daily intuitive practices will assist you in building your intuitive muscle, not weakening it.

Don't Force the Answers

- When we need an answer to any situation, we tend to rush our response. Take a moment to get centered with yourself, to look within rather than looking outwardly for the right solution. The business environment can move fast. Did you ever try to board a fast-moving merry-go-round as a kid? The merry-go-round would spin you right off onto the ground! Intuition works best in an environment that first slows down so you can easily jump on board.

- When two or three employees are standing in front of you seeking an immediate answer on the battlefield of your business, don't force an immediate answer unless the decision is life or death or an immediate crisis. Take a quick walk outside or a drive in your car. Put yourself in a place that feels good and comfortable. Even a few moments of quiet are often long enough. Some people get their best ideas taking a shower, playing the piano, or cooking.

Sleep On It

- Sleep is a deeper form of daydreaming. Our consciousness has an opportunity to play with ideas. How many times have you daydreamed and had an idea come to you? Or woken up with a new idea during the night or first thing in the morning? A good way to prime this is to imagine the desired outcome in important situations before you sleep. You don't have to work out the details; just believe in a positive outcome. It is similar to the importance of using positive statements during hypnosis: "My health has greatly improved," "My cholesterol has good numbers," "I have found the perfect buyer for my building." When you drift off to sleep, your inner consciousness will have a blueprint to create solutions for that problem. When you wake up, trust that much headway has been made. Have a pen and pad of paper close at hand just in case you get some flashes of inspiration right off! Practice noting the progress.

Practice Mindful "Oneness" Focusing

- To start oneness focusing, center yourself in quiet. Close out all external stimuli by focusing on an object on your desk. The object can be inspirational—a scenic picture, a glass paperweight, a plant—or even an ordinary object such as a glass of water. Breathe deeply and take in the object as a whole for between two to five minutes.

Don't focus on the details. Maintain a soft gaze as if you are observing, almost becoming one with, the object. At the end, you will feel more refreshed. You may have received a new idea or approach to your problem or situation. If not, you have started an intuitive process, so be aware of any ideas that come to you later that day or the next day.

- Sharon practiced this with a group of executives made up of a few billionaires and several multimillionaires. One of the executives had been working with her for stress management and thought many of his colleagues could use some help with it as well as getting in touch with their intuitive selves. He had warned her that these men had minds that were "efficient machines" and that she would need to lead off with some fast mind-grabbing pieces of information. After hearing that she was also a relationship coach, they shared a few jokes about working on improving their sex lives and then settled into the practice of whole object focusing. She used what was handy—the bottled water that had been set out for the meeting. Surprisingly, the executives were able to quiet down, breathe, and master an overall focus. The stress in the room visibly dissipated. They turned off their overworked left brains and transformed it into a balance of both brain hemispheres, thus allowing calmness and room for creative solutions to be accessed. (This is the form of mindfulness you learned about in chapter 5.)

Practice Guessing

- When the phone rings, practice guessing who is calling, or when a letter arrives, practice guessing the content.

Give your best hunch to the outcome of a particular business deal. In time your skill will increase. You can have fun with simple playing cards. Practice guessing red or black to start with and then move to suits, visualizing through the back of the card whether the card is a heart, club, diamond, or spade.

Validate Your Intuition Success

- Notice the intuitive hits that worked and write them down. Intuitive messages are everywhere. You may be driving home and overhear an interview on the radio that contains just the answer you desired. You may see a billboard with an answer. The more you trust that your intuitive wisdom can't wait to provide answers for your worthwhile projects, the more you will see, hear, touch, and intuit those answers. Writing them down in black and white gives your conscious mind verification that intuition indeed works!

Your Deepest Dreams Are Underwritten By Others

- Remember that you are meant to seek your heart's desire and to accept the blessings that will support your dreams. You are not alone. You have many on this Earth who are meant to support you, and the heavens indeed underwrite your dreams. Open your heart and shift into looking at life from your spiritual leadership eyes. Use the gift of intuition from your "greater mind" and support it with your wonderful "logical mind." Leadership requires you to use both for true success.

8

Changing Negative Corporate Culture

Control is not leadership;
management is not leadership; leadership is leadership.
If you seek to lead, invest at least 50% of your time in leading yourself—
Your own purpose, ethics, principles, motivation, conduct.
Invest at least 20% leading those with authority over you
and 15% leading your peers.
—Dee Hockand, CEO Emeritus, Visa

Negative Corporate Attitudes, Practices, and Cultures

J ust as we struggle with healing negative attitudes about ourselves, agencies and corporations must do so as well. These negative climates can be as crippling to a company as unhealed personal negative beliefs are to you. Many companies' executives are not aware of them, but most employees certainly are.

Corporate negative attitudes, practices, and overall climates are often unquestionably upheld by their leadership, their stakeholders, and even many of their employees. They are easily transmitted to new employees like a virus spreading from one person to another. Often difficult to see from within, negative practices are relatively easy for outside observers to detect. These practices long ago became "the norm."

Most of us have had experiences with companies like this. Mondays are the worst. Employees drag themselves back to work from a weekend with family, back to the "grindstone," the "workhouse," or the "sweatshop." Mondays are the highest absentee day of the week, the day with the highest heart attack rate, and companies accept it as norm. Callouts are four times more common on Mondays than other days. Often by ten or eleven in the morning, many employees are already "shopping" online or through the classifieds for potential new jobs. Several job listing websites such as Monster.com and others have reported that they have three times the "hits" of job seekers on Mondays, and hits are strongest from 11:00 a.m. to 1:00 p.m. Mondays are monster days for Monster.com.

Government jobs provide better-than-average pay, insurance, and retirement benefits, but many employees complain about the culture. Employees fear retribution if they ask for changes and believe that nothing will change. Many senior government workers count the months and years, even the days, until retirement. Because of excellent benefits, many stay longer than they should, dulling their creative spark when they should move on to more suitable jobs outside the system. These employees admit that they feel like they are "selling their souls" for safety. The government as a whole seems too unwieldy, apathetic, or defeated to make strides in creating a healthier work environment.

The culture of drudgery and pain is debilitating to the human spirit, whether in government or private enterprise. This negative culture is a breeding ground of discontent, boredom, back-biting, and complaining.

The reality, of course, is that such working environments are toxic to our health and spirits. Mondays are dreaded, and productivity is minimal. Fridays are the happiest days of the week, but office productivity on Fridays is actually lower than on Mondays. That leaves many businesses only three days of relatively normal productivity. Of those days, most offices have poor productivity for the first hour and the last hour, as well as the half hour before lunch and the half hour after lunch. Do the math: of the forty-hour workweek, productive hours in the week actually average between fifteen and twenty. Still, companies do nothing about it, accepting—and even fostering—these accepted patterns in the workplace as normal.

Where Did These Practices Come From?

The nine-to-five workday began on the assembly lines of Henry Ford near the turn of the century. Ford and his managers knew how many cars could be produced per hour after they studied how long each procedure took on the assembly line. Over time, the eight-hour workday became an industry norm. In reality, an eight-hour workday is not highly efficient. Most humans cannot work for eight continuous hours, and coincidentally, very few of us actually do. We need time to be sociable, to rest, to have fun, to eat—all during the eight-hour workday. Yet companies still insist that employees clock in (or sign in) and work for eight hours. Productivity usually falls after four hours of continuous work and dramatically lessens after six.

Wouldn't it make sense to pay individuals for productive time when they actually perform work? Shifts of five or six hours with lunch or break times would increase productivity, employee morale, and contentment in the workplace. Some companies are working hard to set new work hour standards, focusing on productivity rather than set hours. In much recorded research, many are finding excellent results.

The workweek is another long-time standard among companies. You can blame Henry Ford again for this business week staple. Ford was tired of losing good employees who worked every day and grew too tired. In an attempt to keep good workers, Ford created the five-day workweek to give his best workers a needed two-day rest. He also invented swing shifts so that his factory would never have to close and he could make cars twenty-four hours a day if he wished.

So the eight-hour, five-day workweek was created more than a hundred years ago, set up for a factory line to accurately predict how many Model-T cars could be made in a day's or a week's time. Why then do these institutions still exist? Who knows? They exist because of history, because they defined a way and time to work more than a hundred years ago.

Our Way or the Highway

I once worked for a company for only one week before realizing I couldn't spend another day there. I worked there as an analyst that specialized in assisting companies to become more profitable. The promotional arm of the company promised a free analysis of business practices, so when the analyst completed the analysis, the high pressure began! The analyst's job was to have the owner(s) sign a contract for our "crack team of experts" who would come in after the analysis and work with the owners to minimize expenses, suggest turn-around strategies, and expand opportunities. The concept was great. The company's style, however, was offensive and high pressure. The analyst was not allowed to leave until he or she had a signed contract for the service. After the first assignment one week later, I was gone.

We've all worked for similar employers, management that is too demanding, work cultures with high pressure, or worse, those who simply don't care about their employees at all: "it's our way, or the highway." Perhaps apathy in management is the worst culprit of all. If management isn't the problem in many companies, the negativity of the employee group might be, which of course is still a management issue.

What Needs to Change?

Strong leaders not only have a choice, but they also have an obligation to find ways to build healthy corporate cultures that do not cripple morale, dispirit employees, and damage relationships with vendors, customers, and communities. Here are a few examples of negative cultural issues that exist in many workplaces:

o   The weekday is from 9:00 a.m. to 5:00 p.m. or eight hours.
- The workweek is from Monday to Friday.
- Pay is based on job title or job description.
- Company structure is top-down.
- Free time is downtime.
- Fun has no place in the workplace.
- Creativity is reserved for "suggestion boxes."
- Management works from desks.
- Exercise is discouraged—on your time only.
- Resting is wasteful.

- Meetings are useful.
- Don't bring family issues to work.
- Raises are annual.
- Pay grades are an established norm.
- E-mail is accepted communication.
- Annual evaluations are accurate descriptors of performance.

Turning It Around

What if, however, leaders really did care? What if fundamental negative practices were confronted and leadership was always on the lookout for lesions of negativity? Wouldn't it be refreshing?

Instead of the drudgery of Monday mornings, what if the company had a group breakfast or huddled for a "team talk," promoted fun, and encouraged new ideas? What if bonuses were paid for solving difficult issues, group spirit was promoted, and refreshing work scenarios were fostered? Wouldn't it be a place you'd like to work? Wouldn't it be enjoyable to have fun on the job for a change and work within a culture that promotes the overall health of the employee group—mental, emotional, physical, and spiritual?

Companies Leading the Way

There are companies that are performing on this higher level of energy. Companies that arrive at this level have leaders who are committed to their own inner work and realize the immense need and advantage of assisting the family employee group to do the same. Without personally committed, competent, and caring leadership, companies have little chance of recruiting a different type of employee group. They will not be able to retain the best employees and will constantly be shifting gears to move forward, only to be mired again and again because they do not have enough committed inner talent.

InvaCare Corporation in Elyria, Ohio, has a corporate director of employee health and wellness and offers a virtual walking exercise program that brings them to the coastline of the Mediterranean or the Italian or Spanish Riviera's. Treadmills and bicycles never actually move, but they take employees all over the world as they get paid to exercise. Their most recent round, a virtual walk along the Mediterranean, ended August 7 and involved 1,600 workers in sixteen countries who walked the combined equivalent of 450,000 miles! The company hosted a celebration to honor the amazing accomplishment. When the local newspaper featured the company and its employees, other companies in the area began to replicate the benefit; now many companies in northern Ohio have the walking program.

Miavita Corporation in New York is a recognized leader in online wellness programs, providing innovative action-oriented health and nutrition solutions to employers, their employees, and their employees' families. With its integrated suite of online and real-world products and services, Miavita helps individuals prevent disease and live longer, better lives. Miavita also gives individuals the tools to make decisions and adopt new behaviors that reduce the risk of diabetes, high blood pressure, and high cholesterol.

The Campbell Soup Company cooked up a friendly competition. It pits factory workers in Texas against tomato processors in California and the folks at the headquarters in Camden, New Jersey. The contest is over which site can get the most workers to take an online health risk assessment. If enough people fill out the survey about their health habits and lifestyle, everyone in the group gets a $50 gift card. Some lucky winners will get a year of free health insurance. And then there are always bragging rights. These are a few of many companies that are leading the way of change.

Examining the Company's Rooms

Redesigning some of the most fundamental business practices is long overdue. The "dark ages" of many business practices need to be replaced. Employees and customers both have suffered long enough in these concrete structures of poor productivity that have little compassion for employees and deeply rooted negative management practices.

To make this comparison, we need to examine the companies in our lives right now and then imagine them operating in an ideal fashion, equally committed to their missions as they are to their employees, much as we envisioned in our ideal homes back in chapter 1.

Family and Relationships

The most intimate connection between humans is family. Here is where our security bond is strongest, our lessons are born, and our deepest loves can be found.

Business has long believed that work and home environments are separate entities for employees. Home life belongs at home and not in the workplace. You have heard the expression, "Don't take your work home or bring home to work." Of course, none of this makes any sense. Employees cannot separate home and work issues, yet most companies actually do very little to help keep this delicate balance. Some companies discourage any personal phone calls, even those that might have immediate impact on home life. Management usually deals with personal work and home life issues begrudgingly, often making employees feel guilty about taking care of childcare or personal home or life issues that overlap with work hours.

Creating a healthy and blended family environment within your agency is an effort that will change the dynamic of the company and start to build upon all the traditional strengths that make the family unit the strongest unit on the planet. Essentially, this is accomplished by ditching the idea that home and work lives are separate for your employees. Listening to your employees and taking an active role in working on a variety of work and home issues will result in successfully blending them and creating happier and more productive workers. It takes work, commitment, and a team approach, but the results can be dramatic.

In some companies, employees are referred to by numbers. You might be numbered by the department you work for or by the social security numbering system. We have bank account numbers, mail box numbers, driver's license numbers, telephone numbers, pin numbers, passport numbers, and untold passwords and access numbers. The company that numbers its employees lacks much of a feeling of family. The most precious word in any language on Earth is our own name. My name is Steve, yet I have had untold amounts of numbers assigned to me.

Consider the human family. It is a group of caring individuals—parents and children and extended adults such as grandparents, aunts, uncles, cousins, and in-laws. While not every family member gets along well with each other, the structure is set up very differently than business. Parents are aided in their childcare responsibilities by the extended family when help is needed. Family members look out for each other, not just when they are together but all the time. Younger family members borrow money from older ones. Adults teach children and mentor them for years. Cards are sent during special times of the year such as birthdays and holidays, and words of encouragement and compassion are not spared during times of achievement or loss.

Leadership needs to focus more on family and can take many examples of how to strengthen their family environment by studying how the family unit works away from the workplace. Companies such as Southwest, Johnson & Johnson, Google, and others have strongly blended family values with work values.

A New "Family" Approach

How can we successfully blend family and work environments much more effectively? How about turning human resource departments into family enrichment departments? HR is a cold and demeaning term. Family enrichment departments offer up a totally different energy. The job of family enrichment is to foster a strong blend of family with employees, not just hire and fire and go to employment hearings. Their task is to offer support to family members. Their mission is to find ways to enrich the work experience by creating opportunities for fun, good health, and career development and to offer generous benefits to the family. The purpose of family enrichment is to promote, develop, stimulate, and enrich the work and life experience of the family by replicating the vital functions of personal families and nurturing their employees in a similar fashion. Healthy families have healthy boundaries, and companies need to aspire to the same.

Employees don't need to be "managed." They desire opportunity, training, development, and the support of leadership. If we can temper management in favor of strong leadership, we are on the right track. Mentoring, teaching, and encouraging others are very different tools than traditional management.

The family unit is not a democracy, and neither should your organization be run like a democracy. Parents are clearly in charge of the family unit. Rules and guidelines are established at the onset of life and usually followed pretty straightforwardly into teenage years and beyond. In most companies, a democratic, free-wheeling environment doesn't work any more than it would work in a family unit. The head of the family is the planner, the visionary, and—in business terms—the boss. Usually, however, families share this responsibility between two parents or the extended family, and businesses can learn something from this model.

First, when responsibilities of oversight are shared in the healthy family unit, discipline and nurturing, for example, are not lost. One parent might be the rule setter while the other might provide plenty of support, caring, and nurturing to the family. Secondly, when oversight is shared, mistakes of autocratic or singular rule are often worked out or mutually arranged. This dynamic avoids the concept that "it is the boss's way or the highway" that many companies struggle with. The boss's way might be the exact wrong dynamic for companies when the boss is not experienced or mature enough to chart the right path.

As in families, leadership is most effective when it is a shared concept. Fewer mistakes are imposed on the employee, or family group. Visions can be discussed and agreed upon or reworked in this model much better than in an autocratic model. Finally, just as we find in families, companies can lose their ability to "nurture" their family members when in a single parent/boss model. I believe this is where companies most often fail: they simply do not nurture and support their family members as they should. The arrangement between an employee and boss can become cold, distant, dictatorial, unilateral, and autocratic.

Creating a Supportive Business "Family" Environment

Trying to keep home life and work life separate is like attempting to ride a bicycle with one tire. We take home concerns to work and work issues to home all the time. The wise company choice is to accept this fact and endeavor to create an inviting and more nurturing work environment that accepts issues from home. Here are some suggestions that forward-thinking companies are using to foster a more nurturing family environment at work:

- Create "family" or "group" time in the company for discussion. In families, this time is usually conversation over dinner or breakfast. It is a time that families use to communicate and catch up on what is going on in everyone's life. Like the breakfast or dinner setting at home, this could be a coffee hour at work or even planning a "lunch-in" for a group of family members at work to spend time with the "parents," or leadership team members.

- Create a support network at your company. In families, it isn't always the parent who performs the supporting role. Often it is an older sister or brother or an aunt or grandparent who steps in to offer support and deal with concerns of other family members. Newer members of the company's family could have a mentor or mentor group they can rely on. This mentor relationship is important for support, friendship, teaching, and learning. In times of divorce or illness, family members bond, support, and strengthen each other, but often in company settings, we fail to recognize this vital area of support.

- Incorporate the language of family into the work dialogue. When leadership begins to distance itself from the term *employee* and use the word *family*, energy changes within companies. Family members do not "write up" other family members; family members support and nurture when they can. Discipline can be constructive rather than punitive. Family doesn't "fire" other family members without just cause or a chance at remediation. Healthy families find ways of connecting, even in times of duress and poor performance. If a separation is needed between the company and a work family member, it should be presented in a beneficial and mutually understood process based upon data and experience. Change venues for the environment of difficult and personal communication. These conversations could be dealt with outside walking the grounds rather than behind closed doors. Interviews could even be performed while walking in the nearby park, where all parties could be less nervous and more spontaneous. The only reason these choices aren't being exercised is because of tradition and negatively held beliefs that could be changed by forward-thinking leadership.

- Offer competitive play. Competition is very important to family dynamics at all ages. When we exercise— particularly when we exercise while playing and having fun—our problem-solving abilities increase dramatically, as does our emotional health. Nothing is worse than sitting at a desk or staring into a computer screen for hours at a time. It is not healthy for our bodies, our minds, our spirits, or our emotional well-being.

The concept of "family" alchemizes the company, transforming the agency into a caring group of family members working for a common good in a supportive environment. A hierarchy continues to exist, but it is much more aligned to the hierarchy in families than the organizational chart that exists in business.

Money and Finances

For too long, the primary goal of companies has been to make a profit. Sadly, even in the nonprofit world, the goal of many agencies is fiscal amassment. Shared prosperity, however, is a unique and more viable concept. When companies realize that the health and welfare of their family members will ultimately dictate the success of the company, we fundamentally change the way agencies do business and the way companies count success.

The 2008 near collapse of the monetary system of our nation almost took America into a catastrophic depression. While economists and politicians point at many factors, the overriding cause of the meltdown of some of our nation's largest financial institutions can be summarized by a single word—greed.

History is full of examples to illustrate my point. Yet most companies spend far more time budgeting for the financial success of their organization rather than the human success. If we budget for human success, financial success will ultimately follow.

Without a healthy attitude about where profit reigns in an organization's strategic planning process, the best of plans can go awry. What if the essential factor for success in any group effort, especially nonprofit firms and companies with a mission of service, was to share the wealth and profits and support those who helped make the agency a success?

Agencies budget funds and monitor those funds closely, but how often do we budget for the personal development of our key family members as part of our strategic planning? As leaders, how often have we measured ourselves not by profit but by contribution to our communities, our customers, and our employees?

It goes without saying that an agency needs to pay its bills just as a family must pay its bills, but how many families do you know whose sole purpose is to be profitable and accumulate wealth? How many families spend weeks, even months, budgeting for the coming year? How many families list as their primary objective as making a healthy profit at the end of the year? Yet in agencies from sea to shining sea, we observe over and over again the sole importance of profitability.

Look to the family for clues on how to build an agency. Notice that families play together as well as work together. Families agree upon financial issues, such as how much debt to have, how much and when to pay for capital expenses, how much money to save, and how much they should include in a rainy day fund, but few families obsess about finances as much as companies do. Sustainability depends upon those agreed upon issues to be sure, but it would be healthier to let the desire for profitability settle into a normal and less obsessive role at your company. Focus on family and on a good work and life balance.

Physical and Emotional Health

A satisfying and fulfilling life is partly based upon how healthy our bodies are. Productivity at work relates directly to how our bodies respond to stress, how we eat, and how well we sleep, exercise, and play. Obesity is an epidemic and leads to an array of diseases and shortened life spans. Our health also depends on management of all the rooms in our houses or "life balance." When we feel adept in managing our finances, leisure, and career as well as adding inspiration to our lives through spiritual resources, we feel healthy, positive, and vibrant.

What if we replicated these most important mandates for a healthy life in our companies? Why have we allowed ourselves to be stuck in small cubicles for eight hours a day with no exercise, no emotional connections, and often the most sterile of environments? How is it that we have forsaken all common sense when it comes to the work environment?

Here are the basic elements most authorities would agree are involved in a healthy lifestyle: play, exercise, a healthy diet, fresh air, adequate rest, and companionship. How many of these elements are present at your company? Play is discouraged. Exercise is limited to walking to the restroom or possibly using your precious lunch hour for a walk. A healthy diet is relegated to an intake of coffee and vending machines with unhealthy food.

Fresh air is usually either not available or relegated to ten-minute breaks. Open windows mean the sound of birds could be a distraction. Air is recycled through powerful air conditioners or heaters, if it is recycled at all. Adequate breaks are limited to ten minutes, if you are lucky enough to get a break. Resting for thirty minutes at your desk or in a quiet room is a ticket to the unemployment line.

Schools are learning that students who are required to sit at desks hour after hour during the day without exercise and time to bond and play with other children are not in an optimum learning environment. Just because we grow older, our best learning environment does not change. Simply put, we do not learn well if forced to sit at a desk for six or seven hours a day. Yet we persist in this sterile, unhealthy environment and wonder why we don't feel well at work or why our companies have poor morale, poor internal health, and even worse, complacency and a total lack of energy. Families fall ill when such important issues as unhealthy diets, lack of exercise, too much time in front of the television or video games, or a lack of money to pay the bills are ignored.

Importantly, the group dynamic of companies works in exactly the same manner. When employees are not allowed to exercise or eat properly, when they encounter too much stress, and when they lack quality and routine communication, companies fall ill and can ultimately die.

Only recently have we witnessed insurance companies—fully knowing the cost of sickness, trauma, and disability—urging employers to think "wellness." Companies are beginning to do away with "sick time" and replace it with "well time," thus encouraging employees to take time off as a bonus for not calling in sick on Monday mornings when they are really just depressed about having to go back to work.

The Payoff: We Can't Afford Not to Change

1. Wellness benefits make sense for businesses for obvious reasons. Employees who are healthy are less likely to miss work, get injured on the job or file health insurance or workers' compensation claims. A recent survey by the Principal Financial Group uncovered some other good reasons for offering wellness benefits: 43 percent of employees said wellness benefits motivated them to work harder; 48 percent said the benefits motivate them to stay with their employer; and 38 percent said wellness programs give them more energy and make them more productive at work. (*smallbiztrends.com/ . . . /employee-wellness-benefits-keep-your, Anita Campbell, March 2, 2011* ⌐)

The true payoff for change cannot be overstated. Happy, creative, and productive employees are a valued resource of immeasurable proportion. There is even greater reward, however. When comprehensive internal change is made, your company will be sought after by talented workers looking for a creative and employee-oriented company. Happy employees build healthy companies, and healthy companies easily recruit the most talented future members for the organization.

Leisure and Fun

Work has a pretty negative connotation, doesn't it? The concept of offering hours of labor in return for money isn't a bad one by any means, but perhaps we can begin to rethink the idea of "work" and the "workplace." Sounds a bit like prison time—the workhouse—doesn't it? For many of us, sadly it is simply that.

There is a real tragedy to Monday morning depression in the workplace. By Tuesday morning, things are usually a bit better, and by Wednesday, the hump day, employees are working at pretty high efficiency according to most studies. Thursday is actually the most efficient day of the workweek for most companies. Employees are over the Monday slump and feel that the workweek is getting close to the weekend. Efficiency is at its peak, and then Friday arrives.

Friday is one of the most interesting days of the workweek. Highly efficient employees come out of Thursday, and the office is actually pretty upbeat on Friday mornings. Energy is high, moods are elevated, and efficiency is good. Then noon hits, and it all crashes down. The weekend starts officially for most employees at high noon on Friday. Most high-level managers are gone by noon, and when management goes away, the cats and dogs forced to stay behind do so as well.

So in theory, the workweek looks like this: Monday morning is lost, having succumbed to deep depression. Friday afternoons are also gone, even though employees might be forced to hang around. So the five-day workweek really is only four, starting at noon on Monday and going to Friday at noon.

Leisure time and some fun can change the chemistry of Henry Ford's workweek invention. Competition is one of those valuable tools. Leadership should seek every win-win strategy it can get, and efforts need to be made to improve Monday morning depression and Friday afternoon countdown.

I find it amazing how little it takes to encourage people and, conversely, how little it takes to discourage them as well. A simple e-mail of congratulations works well, but a phone call or personal visit to the team member works even better, particularly if others are around to hear the compliment being given. For most of us, a name on a plaque on the company's wall isn't as strong a motivator as a verbal pat on the back in front of our colleagues. Any effort to promote some leisure activity or fun in the workplace produces wonderful results. No one expects it, but soon everyone looks forward to the next event— whether it is a competition, an inspirational outside speaker, or simply a called time-out and a walk around the building.

I have also found that time off works far better than a small bonus for work performance. If money is given, consider gift cards or movie passes rather than bonuses in checks. When we get paid, we pay bills, and most bonuses do not get used for the purposes for which they were intended.

Striving for win-win situations means a two-way win: the company wins as well as the team member. One of the most beneficial steps a leader can make is to ask team members to get creative and get involved in solving issues, problems, and challenges and then offer a generous reward.

Creativity is native to us all, but when most of us go "to work," we take off rather than put on our creative hats. When we ask team members to come forward, either individually or in groups, to brainstorm new creative ideas to solve old problems and challenges, we "flip on" one of our most potent resources—creative thinking.

Of all win-win ideas, creative suggestions for change should be the most prized and the most rewarded at your company.

Here is where leadership separates from management. Leaders enable and empower others to be agents for managed change, the pathways to better service, higher productivity, and greater mission enhancement. Encouraging creativity is as easy as getting people clear of their workstations and working on common issues. Contrary to their history, meetings are not the path to creative solutions.

Opening creative dialogue is as easy as changing work tradition. Allow employees to walk, get exercise, have fun, converse, read, talk in groups, laugh, and take a few creative breaks. What will be lost? A few nonproductive minutes at a workstation?

No leader has all the answers. However, if you have one hundred team members all encouraged to make their jobs more productive, easier, less onerous, and more fun, positive change can and will happen.

Once employees know that they can receive valuable time off (with pay) or other rewards the agency can offer them, including recognition, the idea path widens until it becomes a four-lane interstate highway, leading right back to the overall success of the agency.

The Holy Grails of Change

- Encourage fun and laughter. It excites the mind and creates fertile ground.
- Encourage and reward at every turn for every justifiable reason.
- Cut the workweek hours and watch productivity soar.
- Encourage exercise and healthy habits at work.
- Encourage competition, even play.

- Change up the cubicles and workspace. Encourage comfort.
- Allow plenty of dialogue, even nonwork dialogue, among your team members.
- Be compassionate, thoughtful, and caring. Urge your management to be the same.
- Allow everyone to job share, even comanage.
- Use a mentor system to teach, train, and educate.
- Encourage team members to live productively.
- Offer life balance solutions—professional supports, savings plans, addiction and weight loss supports, fitness programs, and counseling and therapy supports.
- Allow pets in the workplace where appropriate.
- Foster lively and varied communication with team members.
- Create a rewards system for everything that matters. Pay is not a reward.
- Think win-win. Keep the company's benefit close to your heart.
- Get the company involved in your team members' families.
- Promote wellness, not sickness (as in doing away with sick days).
- Promote spiritual growth and spirituality in the workplace.

Making the Shift

So how do agencies make this important shift? How do you make the leap from traditional company norms, a life of sterile cubicles, eight-hour shifts, and an unproductive business environment?

First, the environment needs to be changed slowly, preferably from the ground up rather than the top down. Employees need to feel heard, feel empowered to create, and have a stake in the new work environment. Then they need to be given the authority and tools to make it happen. When such change is mandated or ordered by management, it could be viewed with suspicion, even doubt and mistrust.

Ask employees to come together to solve relatively small issues at first. Seek groups of three or four employees who are not well known to each other to meet for lunch or somewhere they feel comfortable. All of the groups can be organized and monitored by a member of the benefits team of the company. One group, for instance, might be asked to review alternatives to vending machines in the lunchroom.

Another focus group could come together to offer better fitness opportunities to the employee family. Taking time off work to walk in the park or simply sit at picnic tables outside for a time would benefit all.

When employees are asked to become engaged, solutions are found. They become energized. When empowered, they become creators. When your agency becomes a group of empowered creators, great things can begin to happen.

One of our local grocery chains in New England is called Big Y. As you enter any Big Y grocery store, you pass under a sign at every entrance. It reads, *Through these doors enter world-class employees.* In their daily advertisements, Big Y shows their family members delivering services, smiles, and good customer service. Their advertising statement is *Delivering goods from our family to yours.*

There is wisdom and thought behind this type of promotion. Whether the grocery chain really delivers this warmth and positive service to their employees or not I'm not certain, but just by stating that they are a "family of employees" who deliver "world-class" service from "their family to yours" is a powerful and enriching concept.

When leadership really gets the concept of a healthy work family and uses all the tools available to them to spread the warmth, wisdom, mentorship, and support of family to their employee group, companies are transformed. Leadership moves from a single individual to a full family of empowered leaders. Powerful change is possible when employees become powerfully engaged leaders.

CHAPTER

9

The Tenets of Authentic Leadership

A leader is best when people barely know he exists,
when his work is done, his aim fulfilled.
They will say: We did it ourselves.
—Lao Tzu

Alchemy has been practiced for thousands of years. It is the oldest science on the planet. While it is not fully accepted in its traditional form in the West, alchemy and its often secret formulas for transformation have much to teach us about becoming leaders. Briefly, it was the forerunner of modern chemistry and physics combined. Alchemists were metallurgists who attempted to turn base metals such as lead into gold through a carefully followed formula using heat, distillation, commixing, and experimentation. Their basic belief was that the most basic elements of precious metals could be found in all metals, for all metals were carbon based and thus connected. With intense heat, they removed impurities from the metal, siphoned the metal off carefully, subjected it to distillation, and then reintroduced it to other "purer" elements in hopes of making a more precious metal.

Borrowing from metallurgy and applying the concepts to philosophy, Rene Descartes, the father of modern philosophy, transmuted thinking in a similar fashion as alchemists transmuted metals. "Rational thought," he postured, "must explain all things for something to be real." (*Discourse on Method and Meditations on First Philosophy*, 4th Ed. by Rene Descartes and Donald Cress (Jun 1, 1994). Thought and reason were distilled to their basic elements, and he concluded that he was alive and that life was not a dream. He summed the distillation up in his now famous quote, "I think, therefore I am."

Fear, doubt, lack of confidence, low self-esteem, judgment, and guilt can be transmuted as well by burning off the negative beliefs we have held for so long that are untrue about ourselves. Like the heat of an alchemist's fire, we can burn off these beliefs by honest examination, illumination, and experimentation. This book has endeavored to show us ways to accomplish this. From reclaimed wholeness, you are now able to practice the powerful tenets of leadership.

Our leadership journey is almost complete. We have taken the intimate walk through our inner rooms following the alchemist's path of transformation. We are left with the truth, with the gold nuggets: I am worthy, I am significant, I can trust, I can succeed, and I will never believe the negativity again. When we glimpse this reality—that our base elements are good and pure, as if made of gold—we step into a different reality, and we become the true leaders of our lives and the lives of everyone around us. We become the alchemists. Because we have worked toward self-mastery, our energy is now free to practice these tenets of leadership.

I consider the following seven leadership tenets to be the solid base elements of my leadership journey. They are principles that resonate with me, and I have made them basic to my walk in life. I'd like to share them with you.

Tenant 1: We Are All Connected

I believe that when we step into the reality that every human is intimately connected to all others, it is a game changer. When I do not see John or Jane Doe as completely separate from me, I change how I treat them, no matter what their behavior might urge me to do. The Golden Rule spells it out pretty clearly: "Do unto others as you would have them do unto you." Why? Because you and I have the same basic core elements; we are just externally packaged a bit differently. When I drop judgment of myself, I drop judgment of you. When I forgive my guilty past, I never see your guilty past. When I heal an addiction, the world moves a step closer to healing as well.

Have you heard of the butterfly effect? The term is used in chaos theory to describe how small changes to a seemingly unrelated thing or condition (also known as an initial condition) can affect large, complex systems. The term comes from the suggestion that the flapping of a butterfly's wings in South America can affect the weather in Texas, meaning that the tiniest influence on one part of a system can have a huge effect on another part. Taken more broadly, the butterfly effect is a way of describing how unless all factors can be accounted for, large systems such as the weather remain impossible to predict with total accuracy because there are too many unknown variables to track.

According to the big bang theory of creation, we are all made up of the same essence as the star that blew up 15 billion years ago. Chemically, humans share 99.9 percent of their DNA.

That's right, 99.9 percent of our DNA is exactly the same! With chimpanzees, our replicated DNA drops to 98.4 percent—a less than 2 percent difference! (CBD Convention on Biological Diversity, SSRN papers.ssrn.com, by P Oldham—2009—Jan 11, 2005).

The human body has between 50 trillion to 75 trillion living cells. Of the 240 or so distinctive types of cells, each knows instinctively what to do by some wonderful super consciousness. A toenail cell replicates, excretes, respires, lives, and dies for one purpose—to grow a toenail. A blood cell travels throughout the body at hundreds of feet per second, gathering oxygen and carbon dioxide, sharing nutrients, bathing tissue, and doing what it is does by some inexplicable wonderful process, all so we can live. The toenail cell might never meet a brain cell in its existence, but it "knows" it is connected. It "knows" that it is part of the whole—a human body, yours or mine.

We are all connected. The Internet is proof enough of how we clamor for connection. I recently found a website called Omegle.com, where at any moment twenty thousand to thirty thousand strangers, mostly young people, are chatting with one another from all over the world. Their longing is the same—connection. We long for it because it is our essence. We are all connected.

When we do not see ourselves as separate from everyone else in our circle, the last thing we wish to do is to harm someone. If we are truly connected to each other, our hurtful actions or anger could then be circled right back to us! When we feel bad about ourselves, it is fairly easy to deflect it onto someone else—anyone usually—but often it is deflected onto the people closest to us—family, spouses, friends. The very people we love!

Leaders who have spent time in their inner rooms and filled those rooms with solid self-reflection, better habits, forgiveness, wisdom, and learning will know not to find fault with those around us who haven't done similar hard work. We were once there as well! How good is it that the employees in our service are learning, growing, and maturing through trial and error?

We have all emerged from the dark waters, and now from the shoreline you have the power to toss lifelines to those who are still in the water. You know intuitively what your purpose is.

There is power in caring. Here we will find our voices, our passions, and our true reasons for living. That special purpose might be to care for the disabled, the elderly, or the young. It may be to advance equality for genders or nationalities. The cause may involve cats, horses, whales, roses, or peonies. It might involve reducing our landfills or saving our land.

Focus on those around you and not on yourself, and you will walk in leadership. You become a "we." We know for certain that if we are to have a truly great society in which to live, we need to do all we can to help our fellow man, our environment, and the creatures within it. Living for just ourselves is a futile endeavor.

The ultimate purpose of our existence is to share that presence, that special awareness of sitting on that rock in the sunlight, away from the river, and to bring that same feeling to the rest of the world. These are our connected siblings, many of whom are swimming their hearts out and gasping for the same presence we are now feeling. As our community on shore grows one person at a time, we become even more passionate about our purpose. We want everyone to find the same peaceful and life-giving shoreline we've found. We have come to the undeniable understanding of one vitally important reality . . .

Tenant 2: Live in the Present Moment

As you read this sentence, take a deep breath. As you breathe in, feel your lungs expand. They are receiving the oxygen that allows us to continue living, that sweet and invisible element in the air that cleanses every cell of our bodies as the oxygen enters the bloodstream and is pumped throughout our bodies by our hearts. See the breath you are taking in as full of little golden balloons and going into your lungs—countless dancing balloons that bring life into every breath you take. Now exhale the breath.

Feel your diaphragm push the air out of your nose or mouth. Continue to exhale and see the air you are expelling. Imagine you are seeing the tiny balloons all collapse and no longer golden in color. We have taken all of the essential elements of the air and are now sending it back as carbon dioxide, full of other gases in small amounts that our bodies no longer have use for. Take one last deep breath in and see the dancing golden bubbles as they enter your body, travel into your lungs, and get pumped through every organ and cell of your body. The bloodstream removes the air now and sends it back to the lungs to be exhaled.

As you exhale fully now, how do you feel? Perhaps calmer, more relaxed?

In this simple exercise we have slowed the incessant voice in our heads telling us to be worried about this month's bills or whether our children are having a good or challenging day at school. Through the easy act of being aware of our breathing for a few moments of time, we are unable to feel any pain of past shame, guilt, or hurt. We do not feel these things because we are not there; we are not in the past, reliving memories of our childhoods or of last year or of five minutes ago. Because we are observing our breathing in this present moment, we cannot feel anxiety about tomorrow's big meeting at the office or what our workmates will say about our new haircuts. We cannot feel that anxiety because we are not there; we are not in the future, imagining what the next day or next year will bring or not bring into our lives.

After a recent snow storm, I dug a path out to my bird feeders, knowing that the birds couldn't find food in the heavy snow. I sprinkled seeds all over the ground and then returned to the house and stood at the window, watching them. Cardinals, sparrows, finches, and woodpeckers came. Mourning doves descended on the food, as did juncos and jays. Within minutes the white snow was covered with birds. I watched them eat, fly into the trees, and return again for more food. It was a complete symphony to me, one of the best shows I'd seen at any movie theater or on television. I was fully present, fully living in that moment.

When we live in the moment, aware of who and where we are in this wonderful cosmos, we can relax and "allow" gifts to come to us. Awareness is the greatest agent for change, and it cannot descend upon us unless we are living in the right now, this very moment.

In his explosively powerful book *The Power of Now*, author Eckhart Tolle says, "If your relationship to the Now (the present moment) is dysfunctional, that dysfunction will be reflected in every relationship and every situation you encounter." Tolle defines the incessant voice in our heads, our egos, as "your dysfunctional relationship with the present moment."(The Power of Now, Aug. 19, 2004).

The ego can steal us from the present moment by taking us backward or forward, but rarely does the ego want to be in the now. It is simply not happy being in this present moment.

What happens when you meet someone interesting for the first time? Your mind immediately starts telling you things: He is handsome. She is important. What are you going to say in response to this person? We are so busy in our unending internal dialogue that we often don't remember a word of what that person even said to us, much less his or her name. Has it happened to you? If we silence the voice for a moment, however, a moment enough to really care about this person, we invariably find someone who is quite interesting.

The present moment is the only time in our lives when things actually happen, and if this is the only time when things happen, it is the only time we can react to those things happening, either for a positive or negative outcome. It could be argued then that the present moment is an eternity of endless precious single moments that all quickly pass and become our past. To reshape anything in our future, we must reshape it in this present moment. This is where change takes place, where we receive our first kisses, our "aha" moments, and our brief moments in life when we are struck dumb by the beauty of a sunrise or the fragrance of a flower.

Living in the present, being more aware of "this moment" is the pathway to peace and harmony in our lives. Any other direction, forward or backward, brings the painful body, the ever-anxious mind, the fear of tomorrow, and the agonies of yesterday.

You can't miss people who have learned to spend more time in the present moment, "the presence." You've seen them often. There are people who simply shine. They walk into a room with smiles on their faces and confident countenances. They have a way of peace and easiness about them. We are drawn to their confidence, to their soft smiles that beam wisdom and inner peace. We want to learn their secret. We like such people often for no apparent reason. We will follow them because they seem to know in what direction they are going.

This is your path now. You are becoming that leader. The present moment is the best moment to start—right now, this moment. Once you have befriended the present moment, life becomes friendlier. You live now and make a living now—a healthy habit. There is a future to be sure, but why live there when we have this precious moment?

This vital awareness of life's purpose brings another fundamental leadership tenet into reality . . .

Tenant 3: Live in Balance

We have used the rooms of your home to illustrate that all areas of your life need to be nourished and developed. Ultimately, success is measured by the state of our hearts and the love we have for ourselves as well as others. Remember the rooms of that inner house we examined in chapter 1? They included money and finances; leisure, creativity, and fun; spirituality and philosophy; career and education; family and relationships; and physical and emotional health. All of these areas of our lives are important if we measure success by the state of our hearts.

I remember when I was in graduate school as a young man. I was newly married and had one small child. I worked two jobs to support my family while studying all the hours I could to prepare for class. Over that year, I was constantly sleep deprived and caught one infection after another. I was irritable and testy, and I recall that every major relationship in my life was suffering. I was living life in a state of imbalance, and had that lifestyle continued any longer, I would have been heading for disastrous outcomes in multiple areas of my life.

It is well understood that you will have priorities. There will be times when your career will take preference over family, but proceed with caution. If you are not feeding your intimate relationships or your spiritual life, the result will be similar to not feeding your body or your mind. It may seem simplistic, but the truth is that if you are not feeding your most intimate relationships, they will suffer and could end.

Living with balance is best accomplished in daily or weekly practices, even if there are areas of your life that are taking precedence right now. Here are some examples of what I have chosen to make important. They might be helpful for you as well:

- **Money and Finances**—I check my bank balance every day. It takes only a few moments, but it reminds me of bills to be paid, how my budget is doing, or if I have indulged in some way, planned or unplanned. I pay bills every payday, no exceptions. I choose to tithe to a favorite cause once a month, usually a different one each month.

- **Leisure, Creativity, and Fun**—Sharon and I have a "date night" once a week. It might be a play or a night at the movies. I also play in a creative outlet almost every day. For me, it involves writing but also a weekly chess match, gardening, feeding birds, or a project in woodworking. My sister-in-law Beth once told me that she and my brother plan a short getaway every quarter. It might be a hiking, fishing, skiing, or camping trip. She tells me that they "always have something to look forward to." Sharon and I have added an annual "major vacation" to the list. There should always be something to plan and look forward to.

- **Spirituality and Philosophy**—Sharon and I have our "spiritual time" every day. Therefore, as I go to work, I am reminded that my day's objectives must also include acts of kindness and openness with others. We end the day with statements of gratitude and visualization of our goals and prayers.

- **Career and Education**—I work a full-time job, so my career gets plenty of attention. I also teach at a college, which keeps me focused on the latest research and staying in touch with my students and their work. But education can easily be expanded by taking an art class or a birding hike.

- **Family and Relationships**—All of our relationships need frequent nourishing. E-mail and texting isn't bad, but Skype and using a camera on the computer can bring long-distance relationships much closer. The phone might be passé for some, but I love hearing the voices of my children, my siblings, and my friends from all over the world. We need to take time to nourish our friendships. Once a year, I like to go fishing up in the Minnesota Boundary Waters with "just the guys."

- **Physical and Emotional Health**—Our day begins in the fitness center; forty-five minutes to an hour is usually ample time to stimulate the body and keep it toned. Good diet is Sharon's domain, and her cooking and vitamin regimen are appreciated (most of the time).

Living life in balance promotes wellness, good health, and a happier countenance. If you have bad habits to break, you certainly know of them, but they can rob your life of so very much.

Tenant 4: There Are Only Lessons

Every single decision you have ever made has brought you to this very moment. We are the accumulation of choices in our lives, and isn't that a wonderful thing?

Several years ago I wrote the biography of a man who became a good friend, Lester Brown. Lester grew up in Black Bottom, a neighborhood of Detroit known in the 1960s for crime, drugs, and violence. While his mother tried hard, Lester was bent on getting some of the "good things" in life—a car, money, girls, prestige, and a reputation. In petty juvenile crime, he grew bolder as he aged through his teens, and by his mid-twenties Lester had earned himself the role of king of Black Bottom. He was involved in drug trafficking, prostitution, gambling, and extortion. He was smart, rich, and respected by everyone who wanted something from him. As his crime syndicate grew in size, his drug trading left the ghetto and traveled to Chicago, Minneapolis, and even Los Angeles. Deals that had started with a few dollars on a corner grew in single transactions of hundreds of thousands of dollars.

Lester Brown had everything he had ever wanted—except peace. He learned to sleep "lightly" and never was without a "piece" or bodyguards. There was always a shadow just over his shoulder, and he never found a truly safe harbor in which to rest. Then on one drug deal in a distant city, people died. Lester's girlfriend, who was part of the operation, was arrested. Trafficking had escalated into murder. The blood was on Lester's hands. His highly paid lawyer promised Lester a quick release, but the release never happened. In federal court, Lester Brown was sentenced to 211 years in a Midwest federal prison for his life of crime and mayhem.

No miracle could save him now, none but the miracle of a change in perception. In prison, Lester realized he had two choices: he could continue the tough road of hatred and violence and join the black prison gangs, or he could really make an attempt at getting it together and make something of his life, even in prison. He weighed more than three hundred pounds when he entered prison. His money was gone. His syndicate was shattered. No one remained to befriend him.

One day, Lester recalled, a speaker came to the prison. Lester went to hear him, probably just to get away from the prison bakery, where he worked. "I remember sitting there and listening to him," Lester said. "He started talking about attitude and how attitudes had gotten all of us where we were—living in eight-by-eight-foot concrete cells. However, he told us that attitude could also be changed and with that change we might know a freedom we had never felt before."

Lester listened. The longer he listened, the more he felt something happening deep within him. "I realized that this wasn't some BS. This was for real. The guy was saying that prison was a state of mind and we could walk from our cells anytime we wanted. Since I lived in a tiny cell and had no chance of escaping it for the rest of my life, I listened all the harder!"

Even the mistakes of Lester's life—almost every decision he'd ever made had been a poor choice—hadn't made Lester a bad man. The choices had brought him to prison, but he wasn't bad. It made sense. It clicked with Lester Brown.

"I remember the next day after my shift in the bakery and when yard time opened, I began walking around the track. I ran a few steps that day, then a few more the next, and a few more the next." In time, Lester could make it once around the track—a quarter mile. He kept it up, and soon he could run two and then three, and then finally he ran four laps—a full mile.

"Man, I felt like I could do almost anything as the pounds fell off me like water off a duck's back."

But running wasn't the only thing Lester started. He started talking to other inmates about attitude and beliefs. He even created a class for his fellow inmates. "You want freedom?" he'd ask. "Then make new choices, adopt new attitudes, and learn a new set of beliefs."

Few things Lester Brown tried to accomplish had ever failed—even crime! His voice and passion were so strong that men began coming to his class. In time, the warden heard about Lester's efforts, and he began to send Lester, in ball and chains, to other maximum security prisons in the state. Lester's message was strong and powerful: "There are no mistakes, only lessons. You aren't bad for your past choices. Maybe you never knew better, or maybe you never had anyone to show you healthy choices, but *you* aren't bad, even if your choices were."

When the governor was invited to hear Lester speak to a group of more than three hundred inmates, he too was impressed. After eighteen years, Lester Brown was given a governor's pardon in prison, and he walked out a free man.

Today, Lester Brown is a renowned and revered international motivational speaker who has touched the lives of men and women all over the world. His powerful yet hopeful message is that mistakes do not doom us as human beings.

"Judgment," Lester says, "is the prison. Lay it down, judge no one, and freedom can be yours."

We have all made poor choices in life. Some of us continue to make the same poor choices. We make them because of deep core negative beliefs: I am not worthy, I am not lovable, etc. Once we drop the self-judgment and guilt, however, the healing can begin. We are not bad people, although we might have made bad decisions. We are not our behaviors.

All human beings, in their thoughts, words, and deeds—whether loving or hideous—are seeking love. Those who commit the hideous do so out of a feeling of disenfranchisement or abuse in their histories. In their way, they are crying out for acknowledgement and acceptance from a higher power. In Lester Brown's case, his essence was good, as he proves every day now. His behaviors as a teenager were based on the history of negative beliefs he had held.

Once we can accept ourselves, the world becomes accepting as well. Once we drop our self-judgment, we find that we no longer care to judge others in the world around us. Once we drop guilt, we become truly free.

When we live with no self-judgment, a heavy weight falls from our shoulders. We walk more erectly, we speak with more confidence, and we realize there are no wrong decisions! None! Everything that has happened to us up to this very moment was for our highest good. We might have made better decisions along the way, but there are no wrong ones, only educational ones. We did the best we could with what we had and what we knew at the time. In accepting this, we stop punishing ourselves and others as well. We see past behaviors that we might like to have changed, but we begin to see ourselves as pure and good. When we live with no guilt, self-punishment ends. We no longer stand in front of the mirror and grimace. We actually look deeply into our own eyes, smile, and say, "You are good." When we forgive ourselves, everyone and everything around us begins to change. We see behaviors in others that might be inappropriate or downright appalling, but we no longer see "bad" people. It is easiest to see this if you have children. No doubt you have seen "bad" behavior from them, but you still see their true innocence and goodness despite their behaviors.

Many times when I took my daughters to a public restaurant to eat, they flipped the obnoxious switch and turned into monsters! Food fights, tantrums, and the "me, me, me" mentality ruled. I disliked and treated the behavior with sternness, but I never stopped loving them. I never believed that *they* were bad; it was their behaviors that were bad.

Tenant 5: Live on the Higher Road

Authentic leadership involves living and working within an ethical framework. It might go without saying, but many leaders really have no idea what mindfulness is, much less ethical mindfulness. The Dalai Lama describes it this way: "Living ethically requires not only the conscious adoption of an ethical outlook but a commitment to developing and applying inner values to our daily life" (*Beyond Religion: Ethics for a Whole World*, Nov 6, 2012).

We don't live ethical lives part time or in certain circumstances only. We remain committed to the development of our inner rooms throughout our lives every day and—when we live in mindfulness—every moment. Mindfulness is living in the present. When we study our breath or the view in front of us or hear the song of a bird, we are living mindfully. But when we are vacating in front of video games or television, we are not living mindfully. We are not present.

When leaders are not present, they cannot be available to their employees or their families. When leaders are thinking only of the future or reliving a memory of the past, they are not in the saddle of leadership; they are someplace else. We cannot create in "someplace else." We cannot make good decisions when we are "someplace else." Most of the mistakes or poor choices we make in our lives are because we are not present in the moment.

I remember the fear I felt when I thought my agency was not going to meet a payroll and would have to fold. Fear takes us away from the present moment. I created all sorts of scenarios in my head. I would be responsible for the loss of homes, broken marriages, and my own loss of career. The more fear I allowed, the greater the paralysis became and the worse the scenarios got. But when I returned to the present, I began to seek solutions. What did I need to do? What resources did I have? Who could I seek out for guidance? In short, I returned to mindfulness. I also returned to a place of ethical mindfulness; there were solutions to consider, but they had to be ethical solutions.

The further we depart from the present moment, the further we go from our source energy, our mindful creative selves. If we go far away, we find the black hole of depression. A shorter distance away we find that anxiety grows, tempers flare, self-judgment rises, and panic and indecision result. This is not the place authentic leaders want to be.

Think of the values you hold dear to yourself: friendship, love, courage, honor, honesty, creative expression, compassion, an ability to forgive, integrity. These values only exist in the present moment—that moment right now as you read these words. You cannot forgive if you are not living in this feeling toward another. Courage, honor, and compassion cannot be displayed from yesterday's dinner table or tomorrow's staff meeting. They happen in this moment. Love is a feeling we feel in this moment. When we feel it, we are filled with wonder and joy.

Living in ethical mindfulness is a leadership tenet. The pursuit of continuing to develop and work on our inner values and how we display those inner values in the moments we live is a key to a joyful life and a state of authentic leadership.

Many of us try to live up to an image of how we feel we should appear or be like. Worse, we try to live up to an image of what other people think of us. This is the trap of adult peer pressure—living a life that we sense others would have us live. This lifestyle has many forms, all caused by a person living in an inauthentic state.

I grew up in an environment where boys were taught not to emote—never to cry and always to control emotions, at least in public. The stoic male was the successful male, in charge of his emotions and able to make decisions based in reason, not sentimentality. Anger was particularly discouraged in my household. Fortunately for me, in time I found healthier outlets for my emotions and eventually found healing. It has been a long and worthwhile journey. This is an important step in leadership, for it leads to the next leadership tenet . . .

Tenant 6: Practice Goodwill . . . Live in Gratitude

What you focus on expands, and when you focus on the goodness in your life, you create more of it. Opportunities, relationships, even money flowed my way when I learned to be grateful no matter what happened in my life.
—Oprah Winfrey

I remember hearing about a man who went through the drive-through at a local fast-food restaurant. Orders were backed up, and although he was running late, he knew that getting upset with the cashier at the window would accomplish little. Then he noticed the car behind him in the drive-through lane. A young mother had a carload of five children, all bouncing and yelling, hitting and flinging themselves all over the car. He smiled to himself. The scene brought him back to years earlier when he had raised his own children. He suddenly felt sorry for the poor women behind him. When the cashier finally delivered his lunch and he paid for it, he asked the clerk at the window, "Do you have a total yet for the car behind me?" Surprised, the clerk said he had the order and the total. "How much is it?" the man asked. When the cashier told him the amount, he glanced back in the rearview mirror, and upon seeing the chaos and the exasperated look on the woman's face, he told the clerk that he would pay for the meal of the family behind him.

I only know this story because the woman called the local television news and reported that she had received a "random act of kindness" and felt she needed to thank the man but had no idea who he was, so she had called the station. It hit the evening news and started a rash of such acts of goodwill all over town for the next several weeks.

When we become aware of each other, mindful of someone else's needs, we often feel gratitude about how much we have compared to so many others. The feeling creates a sense of goodwill toward others and a desire to help. Gratitude and goodwill go hand in hand.

Okay, I admit it: I love goodwill. I work for Goodwill. I love the idea of assisting others, like the man buying a meal for the carload in chaos in line behind him. But when we practice goodwill we are reminded of our own goodness. We feel good about ourselves and any act of goodwill expands our small world into the greater world around us. We want no reward, for that would not be an act of humble goodwill. We want only the benefit of others. In being a person of goodwill, you become thoughtful. An important characteristic of a thoughtful person, then, is goodwill. Higher consciousness, living in awareness of others itself is an ongoing state of goodwill. Goodwill is vital. It is vital to a life of kindness to ourselves, but it is also vital to the world around us, for it creates appreciation and gratitude.

This is a powerful tool for leaders. Practicing goodwill is the way of the servant leader. It is never about me. It is about us. The team becomes the most important concept, not the individual in charge. The time for goodwill in leadership has come. Living in this wonderfully rich fabric of less power and less focus on self, we discover the great energy of teamwork.

Once leaders recognize that true power in their organizations comes from giving power away with a heart of goodwill to empowered employees who are infused with creativity and recognized for their efforts, the leader can begin to step aside. To accomplish this, a healthy dose of humility is required. As leadership energy is spread from senior management into all levels of employees, the authentic leader becomes less and less important until people hardly know he or she exists. His or her work is done as new leaders rise, are mentored, and are given authority. This is authenticity and the leader's finest hour. In Lao Tzu's words, "His work is done, his aim fulfilled, and they will say . . . we did it ourselves."

True freedom is being grateful not only for our rich blessings but also for the lives of our employees and colleagues, our companies, and the gifts given to us by everyone and everything around us. When we are no longer focused on our lust for power and acceptance, we are free to step into the limitless dimension of appreciation for everyone else and their different talents. When we allow ourselves the independence to step out of what we think we are and simply be, we can experience sweet surrender, that powerful act of letting go of our need to control.

What is it we can really control? Can we control the productivity of others? Can we control the environment, the cost of goods and services, or even our own bodies? Truthfully, we have control of very little in our lives, but we can control the choices we make, even if we have no control over the choices of others.

Surrender is a word we are not used to hearing in the world of leadership. Often it is used as a word of defeat or resignation, but surrendering the use of power, ego, and force is the way of the servant leader. Surrender here refers to the letting go of the need to control, and it allows others to open to the doorway of their own possibility. Surrender is the direct path to authenticity, for it "allows" a greater power into our lives and the lives of our companies or agencies. It is the very act of "allowing" that makes it possible for intuition and a higher authority to help us in our leadership challenges.

As a leader, your day will include disappointments. Business deals will fall through, employees will disappoint you, and outcomes will fall short of expectations. The challenge is to maintain goodwill during these vulnerable times and not sink into negativity and retaliation. Disappointment, after all, gives us opportunities to develop patience, opportunities to not take decisions personally, and chances to see the bigger picture. Thinking of this tenet of goodwill should help you maintain poise and calm even in your keenest disappointments. How you react will be viewed by everyone around you. I found that when I maintained goodwill toward business contacts, funding sources, and colleagues, it always came back to bless me. The people whose assistance I requested were obviously watching my reactions. Although they were not able to come through in every request, they often met a future request just because of the goodwill I extended.

As leaders we are often asked for our response to community, state, or national tragedies. Recently after the Newtown, Connecticut, shootings, people looked to President Obama for a reaction. On the evening news, we noticed tears in his eyes as he recounted the events of the tragedy. He came to the aid of the broken-hearted families in a leadership role that demonstrated a deep goodwill for all concerned.

Tenant 7: Live with Faith

I recently saw a YouTube documentary about a twelve-year-old self-taught prodigy who was painting extraordinary scenes of what she described as "God" and "heaven." The concept of God was never discussed in her household; her mother was an atheist. The paintings were full of promise and exploded with bright colors. "I cannot even begin to paint the colors I see," she said of her own paintings. She also remarked, "The most important thing in life is faith. Without faith, you cannot communicate with God." (www.godvine.com/12-Year-Old-Prodigy-Paints, Oct 19, 2010).

The description that best defines faith for me is, believing in that which we cannot see, or has yet to happen. This is not a reference to religion, although faith in a Supreme Being and a life of promise after death can be powerful forces in our lives. A belief that although we cannot see the outcome yet, "it" is on the way to us is an equally powerful position from which to live. "It" can be financial gain, success in our careers, the ideal mate we are soon to meet, a disease-free life, or abundance in any form. We live in the belief that although we might not be living in our truly abundant state, that state is on the way.

Living in this posture of faith overshadows all belief in negative outcomes, all nagging fears about our future, or even long-standing negative beliefs we might have held to be true about ourselves.

For many African American slaves, faith gave them the strength to live. They sang songs during the heat of summer labors, songs that held to the belief that faith would set them free and a better life was yet to come. Those songs sustained them in their hard labors. Faith replaced their bondage and kept them free.

Faith is often found during our most challenging trials of life. A sudden onset of disease or loss can bring many people back into a strong position of faith. Faith is that obscure optimism that allows us hope in the darkest hours of our lives. Faith is a reminder that we are never alone.

I remember as a youngster of nine or ten years old, I believed in an unseen elf named Charlie. For some time, he was a constant companion and was always present when I was confronted with bullies after school or moments of indecision. I felt that Charlie was walking right beside me, and when no one was watching, I'd actually have conversations with him.

"You can do this!" Charlie would assure me, or he would say, "If they only knew how smart you really are!" Most of all, Charlie always laughed and encouraged me to do the same. Back then, everything seemed like a crisis, and if we're not careful, we can grow up and still believe that everything is a crisis. We live in a perpetual serious state, rarely laughing and seldom doing something just for fun.

Charlie the elf was the voice of strength and courage that I felt I didn't have myself, and he was a powerful ally at the time in any boy's life when physical or imaginary allies are most needed. He also reminded me of the importance of having fun, laughing much, and enjoying almost everything. Charlie disappeared from my life somewhere between my twelfth and thirteenth year, just about the time I finally took a swing at the neighborhood bully in self-defense. I missed him by a whisker, but the punch into the air was just enough to get me home from school without Charlie at my side. I had made that giant leap of faith in myself with one wild punch. Later in the week, I saw the bully again and looked him straight in the eye instead of being afraid. He never bothered me again.

Faith is something I believe we all long for, and without it, we feel unfulfilled, as though something important is missing in our lives.

Belief in one's self is the outward manifestation of faith, and it shows in every walk of life. Faith assures us that we are not sojourning on this planet alone. Possessing even the smallest amount of faith, "the faith of a mustard seed," the Bible says, "can move a mountain." (Mathew 17:20).

Thousands of years ago in ancient Hindu society, a great Indian master once wrote: "When you are inspired by some great purpose, some extraordinary project, all your thoughts break their bounds. Your mind transcends limitations, your consciousness expands to every direction, and you find yourself in a new, great and wonderful world" (The Yoga Sugras of Pantanjali). (The Yoga Sutras of Patañjali: A New Edition, Translation, and Commentary by Edwin F. Bryant, Jul 21, 2009).

Finding our passion can happen when we step out of our egotistical minds and develop the faith to care for something, some purpose, some extraordinary project when all thoughts break their bounds. Mother Teresa had compassion for the starving beggars in the streets of Calcutta. John Glenn had it when all he wanted was to be an astronaut and go beyond the confines of Earth. Roger Bannister had it when he ran the first sub-four-minute mile after doctors told him he'd never walk again. Martin Luther King Jr. had it when he spoke in front of thousands and declared, "I have a dream!" Lester Brown had it when he found a way to rebuild his life and the lives of thousands of others.

Those who change the world do so because they believe that their efforts can make a difference, and they live life with a passion that exceeds all expectation, all bounds, and all limitations. Living this way is faith in action. We believe, and therefore, we can achieve anything. Leadership isn't a God-given right. Neither is it a position we attain because of tenure or chance. Leadership is a choice. It is a decision to live in faith and live a life of passion, inspiration, and purpose, knowing that what we do with our faith can and will make a difference. It is a choice to live beyond the average, the mediocre, and the norm. We can all tell ourselves we are just this or just that or that we are not special or great, but it is not the truth. The truth is that we all can change the world. We all can find our voices in the wilderness of noise and chaos around us and emerge to live passionately. We must simply believe it and let that faith guide us. Leadership begins at home. If we seek, we will find our voices. If we knock, doors will open for us.

We shall not cease from exploration, and the end of all
our exploring will be to arrive where we started and
know the place for the first time
T.S. Eliot

As you consciously develop the leader within and arrive at the doorsteps of your ideal home you "arrive where you started . . . and know the place for the first time." You see all the rooms of your house and the world itself with new eyes. In this hologram of your home, you see a vision of the tapestry of your life, every experience a precious thread in its overall design. As you look at this unique tapestry you note the dark contrast of your shadow nature is not hidden away. It simply has evolved into a lighter tone.

You look kindly at the contrast of your negative experiences which led to limiting beliefs. You know now they do not define you. They are in your tapestry of life to teach you—to move you from being an unaware victim to a wise leader. You see the threads in your limiting beliefs having been reworked into colorful radiant positive beliefs. Your unique talents, your passions, your self-mastery are all woven into this wonderful unique masterpiece before you. You are proud of this tapestry and you see that once what you thought was a challenge or disappointment was an opportunity. Your tapestry will never be complete. What you thought was an ending was truly the beginning.

The journey does not end with self-awareness, it begins here. This tapestry, your leadership cloak protects and guides you now as you go forth to bring others along the same path walked by yourself. You know that true authentic leadership is not just being "the boss" it is being the mentor and the teacher as well. As fathers mentor sons and mothers teach daughters, we come to learn that leadership has the responsibility of teaching as well. The healing force that transformed you through your journey now asks you to extend a hand, both hands perhaps, and bring those of your family, your friends, employees and other circle of contacts along the same alchemical path. You inspire this same transformation within others. From a connection to your most authentic self you possess true alchemy to lead, to create new worlds for yourself and others.

You have come far. The thousands of life experiences that are woven into your tapestry reveal that you have taken responsibility for inner transformation. It reveals the person you are today. Wear it as a cloak around you, humbly yet proudly for you are the new leader, truly powerful in the highest sense. The world will be transformed because of you. Begin your journey!

I love Michael Jackson's song "The Man in the Mirror." I think it makes our path clear when we absorb the words and feel the energy. I have the words printed out and sitting on top of my desk.

The lyrics and chorus greet me every morning. They belong there because they are a daily reminder to me of what I need to do to be the best leader, the most authentic human being I can be, this day and every day.

> *Gonna make a difference.*
> *Gonna make it right.*
> *I'm starting with the man in the mirror.*
> —Michael Jackson

REFERENCES

Abramoff, Jack, *Capital Punishment, the Hard Truth about Washington Corruption from America's Most Notorious Lobbyist*, November 7, 2011.

Bryant, Edwin F., *The Yoga Sutras of Patañjali: A New Edition, Translation, and Commentary*, Jul 21, 2009.

Campbell, Anita, smallbiztrends.com/ . . . /employee-wellness-benefits-keep-your, March 2, 2011

Clark, Luke, "Gambling Near-Misses Enhance Motivation to Gamble and Recruit Win-Related Brain Circuitry" Neuron, Volume 61, Issue 3, 12 February 2009.

Chopra, Deepak, *Life After Death: The Burden of Proof*, Oct 17, 2006.

Descarte, Rene and Cress, Donald, *Discourse on Method and Meditations on First Philosophy*, 4th Ed., Jun 1, 1994.

Dyer, Wayne, *Why Settle for Ordinary?* February 4, 2013

Fillmore, Dana, *You Probably Have Hedonic Adaptation Couples Therapy, Marriage Advice*, December 18, 2012. www.strongmarriagenow.com.

Goleman, Daniel, *Emotional Intelligence: Why It Can Matter More Than IQ*, Sept. 26, 2006.

H.H. Dalai Lama and Norman, Alexander, *Beyond Religion: Ethics for a Whole World*, Nov 6, 2012

Hendrix, Harville, *An Introduction to Imago*, May 2013.

Hendrix, Harville and Hunt, Helen, *Making Marriage Simple*, March 12, 2013.

Hicks, Esther and Jerry, *Getting Into The Vortex: Guided Meditations CD and User Guide*, Nov 15, 2010.

Hicks, Esther and Jerry, *The Law of Attraction: The Basics of the Teachings of Abraham*, Dec 1, 2006.

Hill, Napoleon, *Think and Grow Rich*, Mar 30, 2013.

Kabat-Zinn, Jon, *Mindfulness Meditation for Pain Relief: Guided Practices for Reclaiming Your Body and Your Life*, Dec 28, 2009.

McGonigal, Kelly, PhD, *The Willpower Instinct*, 2012.

Oldham, P., CBD Convention on Biological Diversity, SSRN papers.ssrn.com, Jan 11, 2005.

Ortner, Nick, *Breakthroughs in Energy Psychology: A New Way to Heal the Body and Mind,* March 17, 2012.

Pappas, Stephanie, "Why Men Like Petraeus Risk It All to Cheat," Yahoo! News, Nov. 12, 2012. http://news.yahoo.com/us.

Shapiro, Francine, *Getting Past Your Past: Take Control of Your Life with Self-Help Techniques from EMDR Therapy*, Feb 28, 2012.

Shapiro, Francine, *Eye Movement Desensitization and Reprocessing (EMDR): Basic Principles, Protocols, and Procedures*, 2nd Edition, Aug 6, 2001.

Tolle, Eckhart, *The Power of Now: A Guide to Spiritual Enlightenment*, Aug 19, 2004.

www.hayhouseradio.com

www.abraham-hicks.com

www.monster.com

www.godvine.com/12-Year-Old-Prodigy-Paints, Oct 19, 2010.

www.nimh.nih.gov/health/educational-resources/brainbasics/.shtml

Young, J.E. & Klosko, J.S., *Reinventing Your Life*, May 1, 1994.

Author Contact Information:

Steven Mundahl—www.smundahl@yahoo.com
Sharon Massoth—www.thebelievecoach.com